Activating the
DESIRE
to Learn

Bob Sullo

**Association for Supervision and
Curriculum Development**

Alexandria, Virginia USA

Association for Supervision and Curriculum Development
1703 N. Beauregard St. • Alexandria, VA 22311-1714 USA
Phone: 800-933-2723 or 703-578-9600 • Fax: 703-575-5400
Web site: www.ascd.org • E-mail: member@ascd.org
Author guidelines: www.ascd.org/write

Gene R. Carter, *Executive Director;* Nancy Modrak, *Director of Publishing;*
Julie Houtz, *Director of Book Editing & Production;* Ernesto Yermoli,
Project Manager; Reece Quiñones, *Senior Graphic Designer;* Valerie Younkin,
Typesetter; Dina Murray Seamon, *Production Specialist/Team Lead*

ASCD Member Book, No. FY07-2 (January 2007, PC). ASCD Member Books mail
to Premium (P), Comprehensive (C), and Regular (R) members on this schedule: Jan., PC; Feb., P; Apr., PCR; May, P; July, PC; Aug., P; Sept., PCR; Nov., PC;
Dec., P.

Paperback ISBN: 978-1-4166-0423-5   ASCD product no.: 107009

Also available as an e-book through ebrary, netLibrary, and many online
booksellers (see Books in Print for the ISBNs).

Quantity discounts for the paperback edition only: 10–49 copies, 10%;
50+ copies, 15%; for 1,000 or more copies, call 800-933-2723, ext. 5634,
or 703-575-5634. For desk copies: member@ascd.org.

Library of Congress Cataloging-in-Publication Data
Sullo, Robert A., 1951–
  Activating the desire to learn / Bob Sullo.
    p. cm.
  Includes bibliographical references and index.
  ISBN-13: 978-1-4166-0423-5 (pbk. : alk. paper)
  ISBN-10: 1-4166-0423-5 (pbk. : alk. paper) 1. Motivation in education.
2. Learning. 3. Motivation (Psychology) 4. Achievement motivation in
adolescence. 5. Effective teaching. I. Title.

  LB1065.S863 2007
  370.15'4—dc22

                                          2006025879

18 17 16 15 14 13 12 11 10 09 08 07   1 2 3 4 5 6 7 8 9 10 11 12

For Laurie

Spending my life with you was
the best choice I ever made.

Activating the
DESIRE
to Learn

Acknowledgments

William Glasser continues to inspire me with his thinking, writing, and speaking. He remains the most influential person in my professional life; I am forever grateful for what he has taught me and for his support and encouragement.

I wish to thank my friend and colleague Jon Erwin for helping me move this book from an idea to a tangible reality.

Thanks to Melanie Sullo for her feedback and help with Chapter 1, and to Greg Sullo for insisting that I include the voices of students in this book.

Thanks also to Scott Willis of ASCD for encouraging me during the process of writing, submission, and revision. He saw the value in this book and helped me stay the course. Ernesto Yermoli provided skillful editing, respecting the content and ensuring that the writing was crisp and clear. As a result, the finished product reads more easily than the original. Thanks to Ernesto, the editing process was enjoyable.

Finally, I wish to thank all the teachers, counselors, administrators, support staff, and students who have shared their stories and questions with me in workshops over the years. You inspired me to write this book.

Introduction

Consider your performance when you are "made" to do something. You complete the required task, but you probably don't put forth your best effort. Because personal motivation comes from within—you are motivated from the inside out—when someone "makes" you do something, your goal is to get the other person to leave you alone. External control may lead to compliance, but it never inspires you to do your best.

Now think of a time when you gave your best effort, when your performance reflected high quality. You no doubt found the experience to be satisfying. Perhaps the activity connected you to others. Immersed in the task, you felt competent and tasted the satisfaction that accompanies hard-earned success. You might have had some choice in how the task was to be done, or even been able to choose if you were going to do the task at all. It was probably enjoyable and you learned something as you worked. In short, because it was need-satisfying, you wanted to do your best.

In the first task, you were driven to escape the control of another. The result: minimal compliance and lower-quality performance. In the second task, you were motivated to do your best because doing quality work allowed you to satisfy your own needs. In both instances, you were motivated from the inside out.

For over 30 years as an educator, I have observed students who do their best and I have seen students who do as little as possible to satisfy teachers and parents who were trying to control them. In the last 22 years, I've discovered that inspiring students to work hard is infinitely more exciting and professionally enriching.

The job of an educator is truly an awesome responsibility. It is also an incredible opportunity. We create the future every day in our classrooms and schools. It's time to move beyond external control psychology, a model that has taken us as far as it can. By applying internal control psychology, we can create learning environments where students and staff meet their needs by vigorously engaging in the pursuit of academic excellence.

Activating the Desire to Learn introduces a comprehensive theory of behavior that challenges the prevailing external control model. You will become acquainted with research that validates the efficacy of an approach based upon internal control psychology. You will read fictionalized accounts of real-life teachers, counselors, administrators, and students who have put these ideas into action. It is time we gave our children an educational experience that matches what we now know about human behavior and motivation. It is time we created schools that are based upon motivation from the inside out.

Part I

Theory and Research

Chapter 1

Understanding Internal Motivation

Most schools and classrooms operate on the reward or punishment model, and use stimulus-response, behavior modification, or assertive discipline techniques. Rooted in 19th-century wisdom, this model is based on the belief that human behavior is the result of environmental factors. Explaining the impetus for great works of art and other spontaneous human behaviors requires us to identify the shortcomings of the reward or punishment model and to reject it as incomplete.

Given that we've spent a century or so believing that external stimuli explain human behavior, teacher training programs typically require educators to learn how to systematically reward and punish students. Many educators thus see themselves as responsible for shaping the behavior of students by extrinsically rewarding them for compliance. Yet ironically, our system of rewarding students for academic achievement devalues the very thing we say we want: learning. We send an alarmingly clear message, even if it is unintended: "If it weren't for the reward we are offering, what we are teaching you would not be worth learning." In short, a system of education based on rewards and punishment is fundamentally anti-educational.

According to William Powers (1998), developer of perceptual control theory, one of the first articulated theories of internal control,

> People control their own experiences. The only way you can truly
> force them to behave as you wish is through the threat or actuality
> of overwhelmingly superior physical force—and even that is only
> a temporary solution. (p. 122)

Educators agree. Renowned author, consultant, and speaker
Alfie Kohn (1993) notes:

> Fact 1: Young children don't need to be rewarded to learn. . . . Fact
> 2: At any age rewards are less effective than intrinsic motivation
> for promoting effective learning. . . . Fact 3: Rewards for learning
> undermine intrinsic motivation. (pp. 144, 148)

Eric Jensen (1995), noted author and educational consultant in
the area of brain-based learning, writes:

> If the learner is doing the task to get the reward, it will be under-
> stood, on some level, that the task is inherently undesirable.
> Forget the use of rewards. . . . Make school meaningful, relevant,
> and fun. Then you won't have to bribe students. (p. 242)

As William Glasser (1990), creator of choice theory and inter-
nationally acknowledged leader in the field of internal control
psychology, notes:

> What happens outside of us has a lot to do with what we choose
> to do, but the outside event does not cause our behavior. What we
> get, and all we ever get, from the outside is information; how we
> choose to act on that information is up to us. (p. 41)

To successfully apply any psychology, it is essential to have
adequate knowledge about that model. To help you take full
advantage of the case studies that make up the bulk of *Activating
the Desire to Learn,* this chapter provides a comprehensive overview of internal control psychology with an emphasis on choice
theory. I highlight choice theory for several reasons:

  • Choice theory is a fully developed theory of human behavior, not simply a collection of strategies.

  • William Glasser has been involved in schools for over 40
years. His ideas have stood the test of time and have improved
the quality of education.

  • Choice theory is the approach I have practiced personally
and professionally for more than 20 years.

A Question of Belief

If you believe that human behavior is the result of rewards and punishments, that outside events "make" us do what we do, then you are undoubtedly satisfied with our current educational model. On the other hand, if you believe in free will and personal responsibility, then you must be troubled by the prevailing fascination with rewards, punishment, and the desire to externally control others. If you believe that our accomplishments cannot be explained by enticements laced with the fear of being punished, then internal control psychology will make sense to you. You already sense that we are motivated from the inside out.

As someone who believes in personal responsibility, I reject the notion that I have been shaped by rewards and punishment. External forces have an impact on me, but they don't "shape" me. I accept responsibility for my success and my failure. Freedom, choice, and responsibility are the essence of humanity, and I embrace them fully. I share that with the students, teachers, and parents I work with every day. It is why I have written this book. It is what I believe.

Motivation from the Inside Out

Internal control psychology is based upon the belief that people are *internally,* not externally, motivated. Powerful instructions that are built into our genetic structure drive our behavior. The outside world, including all rewards and punishment, only provides us with information. It does not *make* us do anything.

Not surprisingly, students who are subjected to rewards and punishment over an extended period see themselves as "out of control"—people whose success or failure is attributable to forces *outside* of themselves. They become irresponsible. That children develop a mind-set of irresponsibility should not surprise us when they have repeatedly been told that we will "make" them behave, do their homework, learn the assigned material, and so on. Our reliance on the principles of external control psychology has unwittingly spawned a population alarmingly unwilling to accept personal responsibility and to recognize that our lives are largely a product of the choices we make.

The most comprehensive, fully developed psychology of internal control is William Glasser's (1998) choice theory, a *biological* theory that suggests we are born with specific needs that we are genetically instructed to satisfy. All of our behavior represents our best attempt at any moment to satisfy our basic needs or genetic instructions. In addition to the physical need for survival, we have four basic psychological needs that must be satisfied to be emotionally healthy:

- Belonging or connecting
- Power or competence
- Freedom
- Fun

The need for belonging or connecting motivates us to develop relationships and cooperate with others. Without the need for belonging and cooperating, we would only strive to be independent. The social, cooperative instruction propels us beyond independence toward interdependence and community. Schools can be environments where students (and staff) satisfy this drive to connect and feel a sense of belonging. Building a spirit of connection and community is essential to creating a need-satisfying school characterized by high achievement.

The need for power is more than just a drive to dominate. Power is gained through competence, achievement, and mastery. Our genetic instruction is to achieve, to master new skills, and to be recognized for our accomplishments. The genetic instruction to be competent and to accomplish is especially important for educators. Knowing we are internally driven to achieve, we can create schools where students and staff gain power and competence in ways that support the educational mission. Even though students are internally motivated to be powerful, they may not know how to achieve power responsibly. One of our jobs as educators is to teach kids how to be powerful in a responsible way. It is particularly important to remain vigilant about bullying and other "power over" behaviors that can destroy a school. When we help students develop responsible ways to increase their personal power by gaining academic competence, they are less likely to seek power in destructive ways.

As humans, we are also motivated to be free, to choose. Having choices is part of what it means to be human and is one reason our species has been able to evolve, adapt, and thrive. Effective teachers help students follow the drive to be free in a way that is respectful of others. Students who perceive themselves as having ample freedom are not constantly driven to satisfy this need. Conversely, students who perceive themselves as having no choices will behave in ways they think will get them the freedom they believe they need. Too often, their behaviors disrupt classrooms, interfere with learning, and are physically harmful. Educators who understand internal control psychology foster environments that provide adequate freedom for students within parameters that are safe, developmentally appropriate, and supportive of learning.

Each time we learn something new we are having fun, another universal human motivator. It is our playfulness and our sense of discovery that allows us to learn as much as we do. Glasser (1990) has stated that fun is the genetic payoff for learning. The intimate connection between fun and learning is particularly important in schools. A joyless classroom never inspires students to do high-quality academic work on a regular basis. Skilled teachers create joyful classrooms that support the highest-quality academic achievement. When teachers and kids are having fun, learning is deeper and stronger, and students maintain the keen desire to learn that characterizes early childhood learning centers.

Our basic needs lead us to create a unique, idealized world that motivates us. While there is a universal need that motivates me to connect and belong, my individuality drives me to connect with *this person* and to feel a sense of belonging when doing *this activity*. As we live our lives, we create an idealized world comprising the people, behaviors, values, and beliefs that are most important *to us*. In choice theory, this idealized world is called the "quality world," but regardless of what you call it, it is the source of our motivation. Since the focus of this book is on internal motivation, I will refer to this concept as the internal world. Once students put working hard and learning as much as possible into this world, they will flourish academically.

Everything we place in our internal world relates to one or more of the basic needs: belonging, power, freedom, fun, and survival. It is precisely because this person, activity, belief, or value is need-satisfying that it becomes part of our internal world. Each of us constructs our internal world, and no two individuals, even identical twins, share all of the pictures in their internal world. What we put in our internal world is what we are willing to work for. If we hope to inspire more students to do high-quality work, we need to create learning environments that result in more students putting school, learning, and working hard into their internal world. This occurs when students discover that learning helps them connect, be competent, have choices, and be free, all in an environment that promotes safety and survival.

What we call "reality" is the world we experience, our perceived world. For all intents and purposes, perception *is* reality. Theoretically, the perceived world can match the real world. However, it usually differs somewhat because information is altered as it journeys from the real world (outside of ourselves) to the world we create in our head, the perceived world.

First, our senses impact information coming from the outside, at least to some degree. Incoming information is altered because of the limitations of our sensory system. We make decisions based upon what we see and hear. If we don't receive the information on a sensory level, it's as though it doesn't exist, at least as far as we're concerned.

Information then passes through what choice theory identifies as our knowledge filter. A natural human function is to make sense of the world. We are meaning-makers, and one way this tendency manifests itself is to understand the world based upon our current knowledge. Nonconsciously, we process incoming information to conform to our pre-existing model of "reality." Just as early psychologists understood human behavior based on the cause-and-effect reasoning of the Newtonian physics that ruled the day, each of us constructs meaning based on our current knowledge. Sometimes we have accurate pre-existing knowledge and the incoming information is not distorted. Sometimes, however, our "knowledge" is flawed. Skilled teachers assess this routinely by questioning for prior knowledge before introducing new concepts. They know that the learning of their students will be affected by the knowledge they bring to the lesson. We can influence perceptions by adding new information to the knowledge filter. With new, accurate information, our perceptions more closely approximate the "real world." Effective teachers ensure that their students are equipped with the most accurate knowledge possible so that their perceptions match external reality.

Finally, information passes through what choice theory refers to as our valuing filter. We assign—often nonconsciously—a positive, negative, or neutral value to all incoming information, depending on whether it is need-satisfying to us *at that moment.* The more strongly we positively or negatively value something, the more likely we are to perceive it differently from how others perceive it. This helps explain a common occurrence: two students (or staff members) can observe something in the "real world" and come away with very different explanations about what they have witnessed, because values impact what they "saw." Often we assume our own perception is accurate and claim the other person "just doesn't get it." As one wise person commented to me, however, "I *get it* all right; I just get it *differently* from you." When a teacher tells the class they are about to transition to a new activity, students create a perception of the upcoming activity based on their existing knowledge and their current values. The single, objective "reality" of that activity becomes multiple "realities" once it is announced to a classroom full of students. Educators who understand internal control psychology understand that "reality" is more complicated than it first appears.

In summation, we take information in through our senses, understand it based on our knowledge, and evaluate it against our personal values. We actively construct perceptions that we believe are congruent with what exists in the "real world."

Whether they accurately reflect reality or not is essentially irrelevant. We live our lives based upon the perceptions we develop.

At every moment our brains are comparing two perceptions: the internal picture of how we would *like* the world to be at that moment, and our *perception* of what is real at that moment. As we compare, we automatically evaluate how closely the two perceptions match. If the two are reasonably similar, our internal scales are balanced and our life is need-satisfying, at least for the moment. On the other hand, if the two perceptions are sufficiently different from one another, our internal scales are tipped and we get a signal telling us something is wrong.

Imagine you are a math teacher introducing a new concept to your students. You are at the front of the room, illustrating an important point. All teachers have a picture of what a class *should* look like at times like this. Typically, you would want your students to be attentive, to be engaged by the lesson, and to demonstrate that they are beginning to understand the concept you are presenting. As you observe the class, your perception of what is going on closely matches your internal picture. Your scales are balanced. You get a positive signal and you continue to present the material in much the same way. If, however, your perception of the class is substantially *different* from the internal picture you have, your scales will be tipped. You will get a negative signal, and you will change your approach.

This "comparing place" is where self-evaluation takes place as we determine if what we are doing is working well enough for us to be satisfied. I change my behavior only when I come to the conclusion that the world I perceive is substantially different from the world I *want*. The internal signal we get indicating that our scales are in balance or out of balance drives our behavior. In classrooms that use the concepts of internal control psychology, students are taught to consciously and regularly self-evaluate. When things are going well, it's important for students to become consciously aware of what they are doing so they can maintain their success. When things are going poorly, it's advantageous to take corrective action before the internal scales are terribly out of balance. It is always easier to make change when the scales are only slightly tipped and we feel resourceful. If we wait until there is a major discrepancy between what we want and what we perceive, we are more desperate and risk engaging in counter-productive behavior "just to do something different." Having students consciously and regularly self-evaluate is one characteristic of a classroom utilizing internal control psychology.

The subject of behavior has been studied in great detail by Glasser (1998). One of his major contributions to psychology relates to the understanding of what he calls "total behavior." Behavior is made up of four components: acting, thinking, feeling, and physiology. Change any component of total behavior, and the other components change as well.

All behavior, even behavior we don't understand, is purposeful. That doesn't mean it is responsible or effective. It simply means that behavior serves a function. The purpose of behavior is to *feel* better by keeping our internal scales in balance. We have little direct control of our feelings. It's hard to feel better just because we want to. However, we almost always have some control over our *acting* and *thinking*, two other components of total behavior. When we change our acting or thinking, we are changing our total behavior, and our feelings and physiology change as well. Practitioners of choice theory generally focus on acting and thinking because those are the components of total behavior that we can consciously change with the greatest ease. It is not always easy to change our acting and thinking, but it is almost always *easier* than trying to change our feelings and physiology directly. Knowing about total behavior gives educators a way to help students change their behavior more easily, abandon unhealthy emotional states more quickly, and experience greater academic success.

The concept of total behavior is important and powerful. It invites us to take full responsibility for our lives. Once students discover that their behaviors represent a choice they are making, they are free to make more effective, responsible choices. And once they discover that they will *feel* better when they *act* differently, they have a process that facilitates change. The concept of total behavior does not apply exclusively to our students—it's about us, too. The next time you experience emotional or physiological discomfort, consider the concept of total behavior and engage in actions and thoughts that will provide some relief. It is not enough to talk about responsibility; take responsibility.

Summary

Behavior is always purposeful. It is designed to maintain or restore balance so that what I perceive closely approximates what I want. This process of wanting, perceiving, comparing, and acting is never-ending, as we continually strive to satisfy the needs that motivate us: to connect, to be powerful, to be free, to be playful, and to survive.

Internal control psychology in general, and choice theory in particular, provide an accurate model for understanding human behavior. They help us appreciate that human beings are active, not reactive. They teach us that we are internally motivated, not controlled by outside events or stimuli. Internal control psychology refutes external control theory, inaccurately regarded as the "common sense" model of understanding human behavior.

When you apply the ideas of internal control psychology, you create classrooms and schools that are compatible with the fact that humans are motivated from the inside out. You believe "the struggle is not in how to motivate students to learn. The struggle is in creating lessons and classroom environments that focus and attract students' intrinsic motivation; thus, increasing the likelihood students will actively engage in the learning" (Rogers, Ludington, & Graham, 1997, p. 2).

Chapter 2

"Where's the Evidence?"

In subsequent chapters, you will read about counselors, teachers, administrators, and students successfully applying the principles of internal control psychology. Before presenting the case studies that make up the majority of *Activating the Desire to Learn,* I want to familiarize you with the research and results that demonstrate how internal control psychology promotes academic achievement and responsibility.

Each section in this chapter is self-contained, providing multiple snapshots of how internal control psychology is being practiced effectively and supported by research. Use any or all of these sections to bolster your understanding of internal control psychology and to share with colleagues who may have questions about its value.

Goals and Data

Because teachers who practice internal control psychology focus on creating need-satisfying environments, it may seem that data are neither gathered nor respected. Nothing could be further from the truth. Internal control psychology suggests that we are goal-driven and are most effective when we are clear about our goals and intentionally self-evaluate. Nothing is more "data driven" than that.

In "First Things First: Demystifying Data Analysis," Mike Schmoker (2003) writes, "Abundant research and school evidence suggest that setting goals may be the most significant act in the school improvement process, greatly increasing the odds of success" (p. 23). Although Schmoker does not advocate a particular approach to psychology, goal-setting is consistent with an internal control psychology orientation. Until we have clearly identified what we want to achieve, it's impossible to take effective steps. Internal control psychology is built on the process of goal selection and ongoing internal evaluation. Data collection is at the center of classrooms where internal control psychology is applied. In *Activating the Desire to Learn*, you will encounter educators who were successful because they developed a clear vision of what they wanted and persevered even when things were difficult.

Positive Relationships, Mental Health, and Safety

Creating positive connections among students, staff, and community is a feature of schools implementing internal control psychology. Related to the universal need to belong and connect, positive relationships improve the mental health of students. Connected, happier students are likely to do higher-quality academic work as well. Edward Hallowell of Harvard Medical School states, "In every measure of mental health and happiness that we used, the students who did the best were the connected students" (quoted in Good, Grumley, & Roy, 2003, p. 47).

At the very least, disconnected students are unhappy. The potential for violence, inwardly or outwardly directed, is far greater with students who feel disconnected. An unfortunate reality in recent years is that our schools have been scenes of horrendous violence perpetrated by students. In every case where school violence has erupted, disconnected students have been identified. If our schools are to be the safe havens we crave, we must build and foster positive connections among students and staff. Connected students contribute to a positive school climate, one where high achievement is more likely to be reached and violence is less likely to erupt. Building positive connections is important at every level in the school community.

Positive Relationships, Trust, and School Improvement

In *The Quality School Teacher,* William Glasser (1992) writes:

> Quality schoolwork (and the quality life that results from it) can only be achieved in a warm, supportive classroom environment. It cannot exist if there is an adversarial relationship between those who teach and those who are asked to learn. . . . Above all there must be trust: They all have to believe that the others have their welfare in mind. Without this trust, neither students nor teachers will make the effort needed to do quality work. (p. 11)

Are Glasser's words supported by research? In "Trust in Schools: A Core Resource for School Reform," Bryk and Schneider (2003) answer that question: "In short, a body of case studies and clinical narratives directs our attention to the engaging but elusive idea of social trust as essential for meaningful school improvement" (p. 41). The authors spent approximately four years in more than 400 elementary schools in Chicago studying this "elusive idea." Their exhaustive efforts enabled them to define relational trust and conclude that it can be nurtured and maintained for the betterment of students. The importance of building positive relationships and developing trust is underscored by considerable research.

Taking time to create a positive climate facilitates academic improvement. I am fortunate to work with a teacher who spends about 15 minutes every Monday morning in a class meeting where students relate something interesting, fun, or exciting they did over the weekend. The kids clearly enjoy listening to each other, and the Monday morning ritual helps maintain the positive climate that characterizes this classroom. During the rest of the week, the students are actively engaged in challenging academic work. Part of the reason they work so hard and do so well is that their teacher fosters positive relationships and trust within the classroom.

Positive Relationships, Disruptive Behavior, and Academic Achievement

Noted author Robert Marzano is a recognized expert in the field of classroom management and effective instruction. After reviewing more than 100 studies, Marzano and Marzano (2003) conclude in "The Key to Classroom Management" that "the quality of teacher-student relationships is the key for all other aspects of classroom management" (p. 6). The research is compelling, suggesting that teachers who enjoyed a positive relationship with their students had 31 percent fewer discipline problems than their counterparts who did not develop high-quality relationships with their students.

The results extend far beyond the limits of student behavior. Marzano and Marzano (2003) state, "Classroom management is a key to high student achievement" (p. 12). When the drive to connect is nurtured in the classroom, the natural drive to be competent leads to academic achievement. Strong, Silver, Perini, and Tuculescu (2003) affirm in "Boredom and Its Opposite" that we are internally driven by these needs, writing, "As humans, we all strive to increase our sense of mastery. We take delight in developing new competencies" (p. 25), and "As humans, we all share a need to interact with others" (p. 28). The importance of developing strong, positive relationships and academic competence are characteristics of classrooms based upon internal control psychology.

You will read in Chapter 3 that power and belonging are "complementary needs." When we create classrooms that foster a sense of community and belonging, it is easier for students to follow the drive to achieve in ways that are responsible and respectful. Research suggests that community and competence are mutually supportive. The teachers featured in this book intentionally create classrooms that are need-satisfying for students and staff alike. In these classrooms, the internal drive to succeed manifests itself in high academic achievement.

Community Building and Academic Motivation

After reviewing the educational research examining the link between academic motivation and a sense of community, Eric Schaps, founder of the Developmental Studies Center, notes that "a growing body of research confirms the benefits of building a sense of community in school. Students in schools with a strong sense of community are more likely to be academically motivated" (2003, p. 31). Schaps goes on to say that

> students from elementary schools that had implemented the Developmental Studies Center's Child Development Project . . . were found to outperform middle school students from comparison elementary schools on academic outcomes (higher grade point averages and achievement test scores), teacher ratings of behavior (better academic engagement, respectful behavior, and social skills), and self-reported misbehavior (less misconduct in school and fewer delinquent acts). (pp. 31–32)

Schaps calls upon educators to "actively cultivate respectful, supportive relationships among students, teachers, and parents" (p. 32) and suggests approaches such as class meetings, long a hallmark of classrooms built on the principles of internal motivation. Time and again, research supports building positive relationships, a cornerstone in classrooms that use the concepts of internal control psychology. As you read the case studies that follow, notice how the theme of building and maintaining positive relationships is repeated.

The Responsible Thinking Process: Behavioral and Academic Results

The responsible thinking process (RTP) was developed by Ed Ford and is described by William Powers (1998) in *Making Sense of Behavior*. Based on perceptual control theory, Ford's approach calls for students who behave inappropriately in school to engage in a structured process that culminates in conscious self-evaluation. It was first introduced in a Phoenix, Arizona, school serving students in grades 4 through 6. Comparing behavior from the year before its implementation, the following results were noted (Powers, 1998, p. 160):

- Physical assaults declined 62 percent.
- Possession of weapons declined 100 percent.
- Incidents of fighting declined 69 percent.
- Incidents of theft declined 27 percent.

Ford's responsible thinking process was later implemented in a K–5 school in Illinois with the following results after one year: Serious acts of misbehavior declined 65 percent, and external suspensions from school declined 66 percent (Powers, 1998, p. 160).

While classrooms using internal control psychology prevent most disruption by creating the positive relationships that render problematic behavior less probable, some disruption occurs even in the best classrooms. Ford's RTP demonstrates that disruptive behavior decreases significantly when managed using internal control psychology. An intervention process predicated on the understanding that we are internally motivated fosters the development of the only truly effective discipline: self-discipline.

Inclusion

Ford's responsible thinking process has also been used to help special education students in substantially separate settings be successfully integrated into regular education classrooms. A school in Texas had many students in substantially separate programs for emotionally impaired children. Several months after introducing the responsible thinking process, some of these students were able to be successfully included in regular education classrooms for three or more periods a day (Powers, 1998).

Emotionally impaired students are frequently disruptive in the classroom. In fact, it is often their chronic disruption that leads to them being placed in substantially separate programs. Many of these students have average to above-average cognitive ability and are capable of doing grade-level work. Students identified as emotionally impaired have the same basic needs as everyone else. Their behavior, while unacceptable and disruptive, is purposeful. It represents their best attempts to satisfy their needs. The responsible thinking process is effective with these students because it is structured, respectful, and aligned with the notion that we are internally motivated. In over 20 years as a school psychologist, I found that students who are emotionally impaired thrive when given ample structure because they often find too much freedom to be overly stimulating and counter-productive. At the same time, they crave respect, and the RTP helps them choose appropriate behaviors in a way that preserves their self-esteem. Finally, the RTP succeeds because it is congru-ent with the fact that students are internally motivated and capa-ble of making less disruptive choices when taught behaviors that are both need-satisfying and appropriate in a regular education classroom. Using internal control psychology, we can transcend diagnostic labels and teach all students to meet their needs in responsible ways in less restrictive environments.

Choice Theory, Student Behavior, and Academic Improvement

Pease and Law (2000) revealed their findings from a five-year study at Vernal Junior High School in Vernal, Utah, from 1994 through 1999 in "CT/RT/LM and Student Conduct." Students and staff were trained in the use of choice theory, reality therapy, and lead management, all aspects of internal control psychology. During the first year of the study, there were 1,393 referrals for disciplinary infractions. By the fifth year of the study, the num-ber of referrals had dropped to 799, a decrease of 42 percent. More importantly, the number of "Flagrant Incident Referrals" declined from 287 to 26, a decrease of more than 90 percent. Teachers were taught to manage minor disruptions effectively within the classroom. As a result, the number of in-class student conferences increased from 19 during the first year of the study to 1,291 during the fifth year, as more teachers were able to suc-cessfully manage disruption within the class.

Although aimed primarily at student behavior, the improve-ments at Vernal Junior High School were not limited to disci-pline. Pease and Law taught teachers to use choice theory in the teaching of reading. They concluded, "academic achievement rises as coercion reduces" (p. 9). The results of this study are consistent with what has been noted time and time again: a decrease in disruption is frequently accompanied by an increase in academic achievement. In *Activating the Desire to Learn,* you will see how teachers have artfully created positive relationships, resulting in a decrease in disciplinary infractions. Teachers who spend less time dealing with unwanted behavior have more time to teach, and their students make greater academic progress in a joyful atmosphere.

Control Theory, Behavior, and Ongoing Staff Development

In *A Connected School* (Good et al., 2003), author Jeff Grumley discusses his work with students and staff at West Middle School in Rockford, Illinois, where he taught control theory, one of the major branches of internal control psychology. In 1992, after working with teachers for two years, there was a 40 percent decrease in the number of discipline referrals. Eleven years after the training commenced, there was a 64 percent decrease in the number of discipline referrals. This latter fact highlights that when the ideas of internal control psychology are fully integrated into the culture of a school, positive changes stand the test of time. Positive change was maintained because of ongoing staff development and a commitment to internal control psychology. Other studies have shown that gains are temporary if there is not continued staff development. Quick fixes and short-term solutions do not work over time. Long-term commitment and ongoing staff development are essential to ensuring lasting change.

The positive results Grumley noted extended to academic achievement. The initial group of students targeted for intervention was identified as "at risk." After being taught control theory, these students showed a 20 percent increase in their grade point averages compared to the student population at large, many of whom were identified as "higher achievers." Grumley's work suggests both an academic and a behavioral benefit to teaching the principles of internal control psychology to students and staff. Again, there needs to be ongoing staff development and commitment to sustain positive change, both behaviorally and academically.

Class Meetings, Motivation, and Positive Classroom Culture

Class meetings are common in classrooms that emphasize internal motivation and control. Those who subscribe to the teachings of William Glasser and choice theory are especially drawn to class meetings as a way to build community and create the need-satisfying environment that promotes academic achievement.

Leachman and Victor (2003), both 6th grade teachers in Sacramento, California, were scholars with the Carnegie Academy for the Science of Teaching and Learning project when they decided to structure their classrooms in a way consistent with the principles of internal control psychology. They discuss their findings in "Student-Led Class Meetings." Among other things, they decided to "move away from rewards, threats, and punishments" and to "focus primarily on the students' social and academic growth" (p. 64). One important aspect of their initiative was the use of student-led class meetings. Leachman and Victor were careful to provide their students with the skill set to effectively lead class meetings and made certain to give their innovative ideas enough time to work, resisting the quick-fix mentality that often undermines the quest for positive change.

The authors found that the use of student-led class meetings resulted in "improving students' motivation, reliability, and involvement in class activities" (p. 66). Critical thinking and problem-solving skills, two qualities essential to the highest academic achievement, were also seen to improve.

Student-led class meetings are effective because they are need-satisfying. Leachman and Victor reported:

> To increase our students' internal motivation, we simply tapped into their interests and goals, which led us to student-directed class meetings. We came to understand that these meetings create

a positive classroom culture that encourages students to trust one another and take risks. The meetings open the door for students to become motivated, autonomous learners who are empathetic, cooperative, and responsible for their own growth. (p. 67)

Congruent with internal control psychology, student-led class meetings are an effective strategy that enhances internal motivation and inspires academic achievement.

Choice Theory, Internal Locus of Control, and Social Responsibility

The "Responsible Behavior Choice" program, an eight-session group counseling program based on Glasser's choice theory, was used to study internal locus of control and social responsibility with a group of 5th grade students in South Korea (Kim, 2002). It was specifically developed to be a time-efficient approach. A formal experimental design was implemented, including the use of comparable experimental and control groups, randomization of the selection process, and pre- and post-testing.

Data were gathered using Rotter's Control Scale and Kang's Responsibility Scale. Results reported by Kim (2002) in "The Effect of a Reality Therapy Program on the Responsibility for Elementary School Children in Korea" indicate that those students who participated in the eight-week program showed a significant gain in both internal locus of control and social responsibility.

As educators, we want our students to demonstrate socially responsible behaviors. Internal control psychology reminds us that even though all behavior is purposeful, we are not born with a repertoire of responsible behaviors to satisfy our needs. We are born with internal drives but must develop behaviors to satisfy those needs. Research suggests that the "Responsible Behavior Choice" program offers a time-efficient way to teach students the behaviors needed to develop social responsibility using the principles of internal control psychology.

Reality Therapy, Internal Control, and Achievement Motivation

"Making the World I Want," an eight-week group counseling program based on Glasser's choice theory, was tested using a standard experimental design with 5th grade students in South Korea. The purpose of the experiment was to examine both internal locus of control and achievement motivation. The results of this experiment were reported by Kim and Hwang (2001) in "The Effect of Internal Control and Achievement Motivation in Group Counseling Based on Reality Therapy." Data obtained indicated a significant gain in both internal locus of control and achievement motivation among the students who participated in this counseling program based on the concepts of internal motivation.

The study further examined whether achievement motivation was sustained over an extended period. A year after "Making the World I Want" was administered, high achievement motivation was not maintained, even though the students continued to exhibit a high internal locus of control. The authors state, "Since the short term effect of increased achievement motivation cannot be sustained for a prolonged period of time, continuous administration of follow-up programs is therefore necessary" (p. 14). Short-term programs based on internal control psychology do not effect lasting change. Ongoing follow-up and support are essential if we want students to develop a lasting desire to achieve. Earlier in this chapter, you read about the success achieved by Grumley (Good et al., 2003) when he worked with teachers and students over an extended time period.

Achievement motivation is connected to the need for power and competence. To help students maintain the desire to achieve academically, it is imperative to regularly remind them of the relevance of what they are being asked to learn and to routinely discuss the value of academic achievement. It is only with ongoing support that students will maintain the internal picture of academic achievement.

The Glasser Quality School: Academic Excellence and a Joyful Atmosphere

In 1997, William Glasser (2000) established criteria to identify a "Glasser Quality School." These criteria included the following:

- Students and teachers are taught to use choice theory.
- Students do better on state proficiency tests.
- All students do some quality work each year.
- All other work reflects competence.
- Students, parents, and administrators say there is a joyful atmosphere in the school.

While hundreds of schools across the United States have had some training in choice theory, the number of schools that had declared themselves a "Glasser Quality School" as of September 2005 was 21. Glasser (2000) discusses an elementary school in Texas in the opening pages of *Every Student Can Succeed.* The Aikman School, a K–3 facility serving 500 students in Hereford, Texas, serves mostly economically disadvantaged children, only 20 percent of whom speak English when they begin school. In 2000, after fully infusing choice theory into the school, all Aikman students passed the Texas Assessment of Academic Skills (TAAS) in English at the 90th percentile or higher (Glasser, 2000). Prior to becoming immersed in the ideas of choice theory, students at the Aikman School fared poorly on the TAAS. While schools that operate using internal control psychology tend not to be overly focused on high-stakes testing, their students do well on these tests. As the criteria for a Glasser Quality School suggest, the school is not only a joyful place; it is a place where students succeed academically. When educators ask for evidence that internal control psychology is effective, they need only look at schools that have made a commitment to apply these concepts intentionally and remain dedicated to the concepts of self-evaluation and continuous improvement.

Lead Management and Collaboration

In the fall of 1997, the School of Education (SOE) at Indiana University Northwest in Gary, Indiana, underwent a review by the National Council for Accreditation of Teacher Education (NCATE). The SOE did not meet a single standard. The NCATE took note of the adversarial relationship among faculty. Morale was horrendous.

A new dean was hired for the SOE in January 1999, and he adopted internal control psychology as his leadership model to improve the effectiveness of the department. Trained in reality therapy, the dean utilized the "lead management" approach advocated by William Glasser, creator of choice theory psychology. The results of his efforts are detailed by Wigle and Sandoval (2000) in "Change and Challenges in a School of Education: Choice Theory as an Effective Leadership Paradigm":

> Over 15 months, the SOE made enormous progress. The adversarial atmosphere among the faculty was replaced with one of mutual respect and collaborative behaviors. The faculty initiated significant, meaningful, and lasting changes that enabled their programs to truly prepare educational professionals for the 21st century. Not incidentally, in an accreditation visit in April, 2001, the SOE was found to have met all 20 NCATE standards. (p. 8)

Leading a staff is not unlike leading a classroom. All staff members have their ideas about how the school should operate. Internal control psychology teaches us that these internal pictures drive us. One essential skill of a leader is to forge a shared vision. The SOE at Indiana University Northwest was typical of many schools and classrooms. It was characterized by multiple internal pictures and pulled in multiple directions. The results were predictable and speak for themselves: adversarial relationships and a failure to meet expected standards. Under the guidance of a skilled leader using the principles of internal control psychology, the SOE was able to develop the shared internal picture needed to achieve quality. A disheartening situation was turned around in less than a year and a half. If the staff had not been engaged, there is little doubt they would have continued to struggle. A management approach that relied on bossing and coercing would not have resulted in the creation of the shared vision that helped the SOE succeed.

Leadership based on internal control psychology brings out the best in a staff, whether at a university, a high school, a middle school, or an elementary school. Teachers who work with students to develop a shared picture will inspire students to do the highest-quality academic work. With internal control psychology, collaboration replaces coercion, and dramatic improvement often follows.

Summary

The evidence is substantial and impressive. From formalized programs based on choice theory in Utah (Pease & Law, 2000) and perceptual control theory in Arizona and Texas (Powers, 1998), to experimental studies undertaken in South Korea (Kim, 2002), to reports on the effectiveness of control theory training in Illinois (Good et al., 2003), to examining the effects of choice theory on leadership in Indiana (Wigle & Sandoval, 2000), to more than 100 independent studies reviewed by Marzano and Marzano (2003) and others, it is clear that schools that employ the concepts of internal control psychology have fewer disruptive behaviors and students who do better academically than before. As coercion is reduced and educators create need-satisfying environments, schools are transformed into the learning communities we want.

The reward/punishment paradigm, based on coercion and fear, has a ceiling of compliance. To achieve the highest quality learning, we need a model that is congruent with internal control psychology, a model that respects human beings as the active, goal-driven, internally motivated beings that we are. Time and again, research suggests that when we are discussing the highest levels of achievement, we are driven from the inside out. When we create classrooms and schools built on the principles of internal control psychology, we give our students a chance to excel and foster excellence in education.

The chapters that follow tell the stories of classroom teachers, counselors, administrators, and students. Each demonstrates internal control psychology in action. The specifics differ because they involve students of different ages and adults in different roles, but each of these stories shows that we are truly motivated from the inside out.

Part II

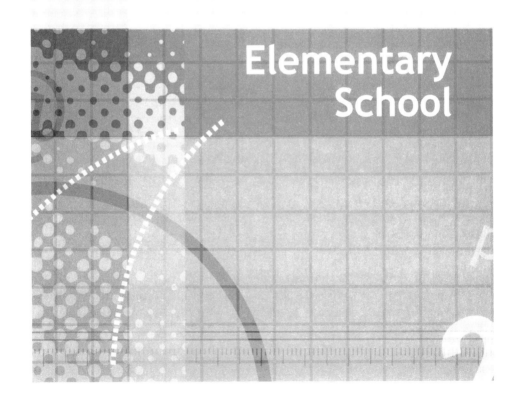

Elementary School

Chapter 3

Competition Is as Important as Cooperation

Pam has taught in the primary grades for eight years, the past five in 1st grade. Even before she became familiar with internal control psychology, she considered herself a skilled teacher. Her greatest strength, she believes, is creating a caring community with her kids. Prior to hearing about internal control psychology, Pam had a clear vision of what her class should look like. Her goal was to create an environment that was full of joy, laughter, and excitement. Pam's priority was to get kids to love school so they would immerse themselves in the more rigorous academics that would face them as they moved through the grades.

Pam's district offered a summer workshop about internal motivation. A few of her friends from the elementary school were going to be part of the group, and it sounded interesting. During the first day, the group was learning about the basic needs that drive behavior. Pam assumed the needs were relatively equal in strength until they did an activity examining the strength of each need. Not surprisingly, Pam discovered that she is a "belonging and connecting" person. Although Pam is driven by all of the needs, her need to connect and belong is especially strong.

During the workshop, participants began to look at how to put the concepts of internal motivation to work in their classrooms. One activity asked participants to look at everything they asked kids to do during a certain time frame, like a particular morning or afternoon. Participants were then asked to determine what need or needs the kids could easily meet by doing what they were asked to do. The instructor said, "Remember that all behavior is purposeful. We act to satisfy our needs. If you create a classroom where kids can satisfy their needs by doing what you want them to do, they will almost always do what you ask. On the other hand, if the only way kids can meet their needs is by doing *something else,* they'll be much more likely to engage in what you might call 'misbehavior.'"

At that point, Pam asked, "Isn't it 'misbehavior' when kids are doing something they shouldn't do in a classroom?"

"You can call it 'misbehavior' if you want," her instructor said. "I try not to use that term. When I call something 'misbehavior,' I see it negatively. By extension, I might perceive the child negatively, so I just call it 'behavior.' Like all behavior, this action is purposeful. It's engaged in to meet some need."

"Are you saying we should accept the behavior just because it's purposeful?" Pam asked.

"Not at all. But it's helpful for me to remember that the behavior isn't random or engaged in simply to be defiant. It's done to satisfy a need."

"So what should we do?"

"I suggest intentionally creating an environment that makes it easy for kids to meet all their needs by doing what you want. If they can satisfy their needs by doing what you ask, there's virtually no reason not to cooperate. In fact, it's counterproductive to behave otherwise. 'Misbehavior,' to use your term, creates internal conflict by interfering with the drive to belong and cooperate. That's why you get so little unwanted behavior in a need-satisfying classroom."

"Do you think we can eliminate *all* misbehavior?" Pam asked.

"In every classroom, there will be some upset and disruption. But in a need-satisfying situation, students are naturally motivated to resolve problems quickly."

"Will you give us an example?" Pam asked.

"Sure," the instructor answered, "but I'd like to begin by using an example from outside of school. I want you to think about one of your good friends. Do you and this good friend ever argue?"

"Of course, we argue from time to time. There are times when we see things differently. We're friends but we're not identical."

"Exactly. And when these occasional arguments or disagreements come up, do you think about terminating the friendship?"

"Of course not!" Pam answered. "That's crazy. While I don't like to argue, I'd never let a disagreement ruin an important friendship. No one with a strong friendship would."

"Would it be fair to say that friends want to work things out because they value the relationship, even though they're in the midst of a disagreement?"

"That seems like a reasonable enough description."

"Exactly. Even in the best relationships, like a strong friendship, there will be arguments and upset. It's inevitable anytime you get two or more people together. Since you can't possibly want the same thing all the time, conflict is inevitable. But because the friendship is need-satisfying, you are motivated to resolve your differences quickly and respectfully. Do you agree?"

"Yes," said Pam. "It's hard to imagine an argument that would be so overwhelming as to destroy an important friendship."

"OK, Pam. Now I want you to consider a relationship that is not especially need-satisfying. Imagine someone you need to interact with, perhaps at work, someone you don't especially like. Working together on some project, you have an argument. Would it be the same?"

"Absolutely not," Pam said. "Even a trivial argument would make me want to get as far away from that person as possible!"

"Thanks, Pam. Now let's bring this to the classroom. If kids see the classroom as a place where they can generally satisfy their needs by doing what you want, you'll still have the occasional disruption and problem. Even best friends argue from time to time. But just as good friends are motivated to quickly and respectfully resolve their differences, kids who disrupt in a need-satisfying environment will be motivated to resolve the trouble quickly and relatively easily."

"But if the classroom isn't need-satisfying for the kid—" Pam began.

"Then what, Pam?" her instructor asked.

"Then there's no motivation to end the problem. In fact, kids may be getting a lot of their needs met by misbehaving and disrupting. Especially the needs for freedom and power."

• • •

Pam found the discussion interesting, but it wasn't something she related to on a personal level. Working with 1st graders, she really didn't have many behavioral problems—what she called "misbehavior." Pam didn't think much more about that discussion until a couple of months later when she was in a discussion group at her school. Five or six teachers would get together regularly to talk about what they were doing in their classrooms to foster internal motivation and responsibility. They usually didn't spend a lot of time talking about disruption and other problem behaviors. They had decided to focus on the positive and share what they were doing to promote internal motivation. Still, the group wanted to talk about how they managed disruption one day, so they spent some time on this topic.

During the discussion, someone asked Pam how she managed disruption in her classroom. Pam replied, "Because I work with the little ones, I don't have a lot of disruption. When it does happen, it's usually because someone doesn't want to share, or one child is bossing another child, or one child doesn't want to work with a classmate who has asked him or her to be in their group. Little things like that."

"Pam," someone asked, "what needs do you think those situations involve?"

"Freedom and power," Pam said. Everyone agreed. "The strategy that seems to always work for me is to redirect the upset or misbehaving child. I put a special emphasis on belonging and creating a caring community. As soon as I see power and freedom getting in the way, I redirect the children to something that is fun and that connects us. They usually forget about the problem in a matter of a few seconds and calm is restored."

At the end of the discussion, one of Pam's colleagues asked her if she had ever read *Peaceful Parenting* by Nancy Buck. "Pam," she said. "I'd like to lend you a copy. I think it will give you another way to look at things. I'll be especially interested in what you think about the idea of 'complementary needs.'"

What Pam read gave her a new way of conceptualizing the needs. Buck (2000) suggests that psychological needs fall into two groups. She calls belonging and fun the cooperative needs. Power and freedom are referred to as the competitive needs. During our lives, we cycle through phases where one set of needs—cooperative or competitive—tends to take precedence. It's not that the other needs disappear. It's just that one pair or the other tends to dominate during different developmental phases. Most kids in the 1st grade are primarily driven by the cooperative needs of belonging and fun. When Pam read this, it dawned on her why she is so happy in her classroom! As someone who emphasizes community and fun, there's a natural match between what Pam values and where the kids are developmentally.

Pam also understood why redirecting was so successful. When her usually cooperative kids ventured into the competitive realm dominated by power and freedom, Pam usually got them back quickly by focusing on their dominant needs of belonging and fun. But there's a price to pay for this short-term success.

To become a successful, effective adult, we need to learn how to compete as well as how to cooperate. We're born with basic needs, but we aren't born with behaviors to satisfy our needs responsibly. What Pam realized as she read *Peaceful Parenting* is that she was passing up the chance to teach her kids how to be competitive in a fair, respectful way. Every time they moved into the competitive domain, she redirected them to the cooperative. Since they were dominated by the need to cooperate, they were easily redirected. While it was "successful," Pam realized that she was missing a great opportunity to teach.

People who don't learn how to compete effectively and responsibly can become bullies, those who will do anything to achieve power. They can grow into adults who don't fight fairly and hurt people who get in their way. Others who don't learn to compete effectively can grow into adults who will avoid competition and conflict at all costs. Because they have compensated by developing wonderful connecting skills, they'll do everything possible to smooth things over, resolve conflict, and keep the peace, even if it means they are treated unfairly in the process.

Pam realized that she was unintentionally creating an environment where kids didn't practice appropriate competitive behaviors. Even though the competitive needs sometimes bring more turbulence, Pam believed it was her responsibility to help kids learn how to meet all of their needs in appropriate, prosocial ways. Pam had been unconsciously sending out an unintended message to her students: cooperation is good and competition is bad. In fact, the needs are complementary. All are essential. Pam had only given her attention to one side of the coin. She was determined to honor the other side as well.

When her discussion group met a few weeks later, Pam was excited to share her learning. "After reading *Peaceful Parenting*," she said, "I see the needs as complementary. I have a new way to look at behaviors designed to get freedom and power, especially in disruptive ways."

"Will you elaborate, Pam?" someone asked.

"It is much easier to deal with kids when they are using cooperative behaviors instead of competitive behaviors. Until recently, I was comfortable redirecting the kids back into the cooperative domain. Now I see that they need to learn how to be respectfully competitive, and if I don't help them learn how, I'm not doing everything I can to help them become whole."

"Do you have any idea how you are going to go about this, Pam?"

"Well," she said, "I got one especially helpful suggestion from the book. I've already used it a few times and it has really worked well. When a child disrupts or breaks a classroom rule, instead of redirecting the child, now I say, 'What was it you wanted to get when you . . . ?' It's amazing! Because I really do have good relationships with my kids, they tell me! Then I ask, 'If we can figure out a way for you to get what you want without breaking the rules, would that be worth learning?' Again, it works! The kids are receptive because I'm helping them get what they want. I'm happier because I'm helping them learn how to satisfy their competitive needs in respectful, responsible ways. I know I still have a lot to learn, but I feel as if I've made a major discovery. Who knows? Maybe someday I'll even stop calling it 'misbehavior'!"

Commentary

Like many elementary school teachers, Pam skillfully created a caring community. Students feel a sense of connection and belonging in such an environment. Because young children are especially driven by the need to belong, Pam had few discipline problems. When the students behaved inappropriately, Pam redirected them, taking advantage of their innate desire to cooperate. For example, a child who was getting too boisterous in a group was unobtrusively invited to play a favorite game at the computer, where he could work independently without disrupting others. The disruption was quelled, but Pam missed an opportunity to teach her students how to behave appropriately in a cooperative learning activity.

As she became familiar with internal control psychology, Pam learned that the four psychological needs are complementary. The competitive needs (power, freedom) are as important as the cooperative needs (belonging, fun). Until Pam discovered this, she practiced the redirecting strategies that most teachers use.

What's wrong with such a "common sense" approach? All behavior is purposeful, engaged in to meet a need. When a student tries to achieve power and is redirected toward something that meets the need for belonging, the power need remains unmet. Unless students are taught how to meet their needs responsibly, they will continue to act inappropriately and often interfere with the learning of others every time they try to gain power.

Students in the cooperative phase still need power and freedom. Driven by the cooperative needs, they are especially receptive to adult instruction and assistance. This is the ideal time to help students develop a foundation of behaviors to achieve power and freedom in appropriate ways. Because Pam emphasized relationships and created a caring community, she could help her students develop respectful competitive behaviors. Once Pam realized this, she saw that she had many opportunities to help her young students develop power and freedom behaviors that were appropriate and responsible.

Pam identified herself as having a strong need for belonging. It is worthwhile for teachers to assess the strength of their own needs. Often they discover they have nonconsciously structured a classroom that reflects their own orientation. For example, teachers with a strong need for freedom create classrooms with lots of options. Students with need profiles that are compatible with their teachers' profiles do very well in that setting. Students whose need profiles are different often struggle. The most successful teachers structure a learning environment in which all the need areas are addressed so students can satisfy all their needs by doing what their teachers ask. Such classrooms are characterized by high achievement and minimal disruption.

What You Can Do

• Remember that the psychological needs are complementary.

• Remember that children in the cooperative phase still need power and freedom and are particularly receptive to adult assistance.

• Teach students how to meet their needs responsibly instead of simply redirecting them when they behave inappropriately. Redirection is a short-term solution. Equipping students with new, appropriate behaviors is beneficial over time.

• Structure a classroom where students can satisfy their needs by doing what you want. There will be less disruption, maximizing time for learning and achievement.

• Intentionally create lesson plans that easily allow students to connect, achieve, choose, and have fun in a safe environment as they immerse themselves in the activities you have designed.

- Create the caring community found in most primary grade classrooms. Academic success is directly related to the quality of the relationships you create.

Chapter 4

Helping Students Value Learning

Jen had been an elementary school counselor for five years when she learned about internal control psychology in an in-depth way. The ideas of internal motivation and control were touched upon only peripherally when she was in graduate school. Most of the professors and the texts they selected emphasized behavior modification. When her school district offered a workshop about internal motivation, she enrolled.

What first impressed Jen about the workshop was the emphasis on building a positive relationship. She sees herself as a "people person" and has always connected easily with kids. That ability never seemed especially valued in her coursework, which was more focused on charting behavior and developing fixed or interval schedules of reinforcement to bring about improved behavior. Jen became skilled at applying external control psychology.

Before taking this workshop, Jen would have said she "naturally" connected well with others. But her instructor challenged her: "Jen, you don't 'naturally' connect with kids. You have a strong need for belonging, but that doesn't make you 'naturally' good at connecting. Think about all the socially unskilled kids you've worked with. Many of them have a strong need for belonging, but they haven't developed the behaviors to connect comfortably with others. Because you've internalized so many socially effective behaviors, you have tricked yourself into thinking that you are just 'naturally' good with people. You deserve more credit. Your ability to build positive relationships with kids is the result of a strong need for belonging coupled with the effective behaviors you've developed."

That comment captured something Jen values about looking at life from the inside out: the emphasis on taking responsibility for our lives, owning the successes as well as the struggles. She now sees herself as someone who deserves credit for developing the behaviors that help her build strong relationships with others, including the students in her school.

Even though a lot of internal control psychology made sense to Jen, there was one concept she resisted. At the beginning of the workshop, she was told that we are born with basic needs and that we are internally motivated from birth. Jen believed that adults and adolescents are internally motivated, and she understood the importance of giving kids lots of freedom and power in school when they get older. But as an elementary school counselor, she had had success with well-structured behavior modification programs. Kids seemed to love the rewards, and as a result, they did better in school. It seemed to Jen that kids were born externally motivated and developed internal motivation during adolescence.

About six months after the workshop, Jen told one of her colleagues that she was struggling with the idea that young kids were internally motivated. Though she was intrigued by the concept of internal motivation, her experience suggested that she could motivate young kids with rewards.

Her friend Brenda, a teacher in another elementary school, had been in the workshop with her. Jen decided to talk with Brenda because she liked and respected her. "You know this whole thing about how we are internally motivated from birth? If that's the case, how come I can motivate kids using external rewards? Brenda, I haven't given up rewarding my students. It works!"

"Jen, it's OK with me if you use incentive programs and reward your counselees. In the workshop, we were simply invited to use ideas that we thought would work better than what we had done in the past."

"What do you think about rewarding kids?" Jen asked. "You seemed enthusiastic about going in a different direction."

"I think rewarding kids for learning is harmful, but I understand why you are hanging on to your reward systems," Brenda answered.

"I'm confused," Jen said. "How can you understand my use of rewards when you think they're counterproductive?"

Brenda responded, "Forget the kids for a minute. Look at your motivation. What do *you* want?"

"That's easy," Jen answered. "I want the kids to be productive in school. I want them to develop a work ethic. I want them to behave appropriately."

Brenda asked, "Did you try to get what you want without rewards?"

"Yes!" Jen practically shouted. "That's the whole point! Every time I give up external rewards, the kids' behavior deteriorates. When I use external rewards, I get better results! God, this is so frustrating!"

"Hang on a second, Jen. It makes perfect sense. Remember when you used to say you were 'naturally' good at creating positive relationships?"

"Of course. It wasn't that long ago," Jen replied. "Then I discovered that I had developed a collection of effective behaviors over time. That it wasn't just 'natural.'"

"Exactly," said Brenda. "Jen, you built that repertoire over a period of years. Even though you didn't decide to be a counselor until about 10 years ago, you've been creating 'relationship behaviors' since you were a kid. You've had lots of practice."

"What's your point?" Jen asked.

"Simply that you're relatively new in the practice of tapping into internal motivation. You've been at this for less than a year. It makes sense that you haven't yet developed a whole repertoire of behaviors relating to internal control. Remember, Jen, that *you* are internally motivated. If the rewards you have been using seem to help you be more successful as a counselor, then of course you continue to use them! As soon as you stop rewarding the kids, you feel lost because you still have a job to do but you no longer have your tools."

"Let me get this straight. I have a vision of what I want as a counselor. I have my 'behavior mod' tools that work well. If that's the case, why would I ever abandon what works?"

Brenda paused. "If you were *really* convinced that rewards worked to your satisfaction, you would have stopped studying internal motivation soon after our workshop. On some level you must believe that implementing behavior mod plans won't help you get what *you* want."

After a few moments of silence, Brenda continued, "Pick a kid you've been working with. Let's talk about him or her and find out if you're satisfied with rewarding, and we'll decide if this kid is internally or externally motivated."

"OK," Jen said. "Let's talk about Paul. He's an under-achiever."

"Tell me about him."

"He's a sweet kid. Very likeable. He doesn't cause problems in his classroom. He's in the 4th grade. He gets along well with peers. He just doesn't put in a great deal of effort in school. You know that 4th grade is a critical year and that there are increased academic demands. The teachers are afraid that if Paul doesn't start to perform better, he'll fall behind his classmates. And they worry that if he gets behind he'll develop into a behavior problem."

"What have you done so far with Paul?"

"His teachers and I have created a simple behavior mod system. When Paul stays productive and on task for a specified time period, he earns some time with me. He gets to choose what we do as long as it is within reason. Usually, he asks me to bring him to the gym to play basketball. Other times, he asks to play games on the computer in my office."

"Would you say it's working?" Brenda asked.

"Absolutely. The teachers report that Paul is considerably more productive since we began the incentive program."

"So the teachers think it's working. What about Paul? What does he think?"

"To be truthful, I've never asked him. When he earns time with me, I praise him and ask him what he'd like to do. Like I said, he usually wants to go to the gym or play a game on the computer."

"Does Paul seem bothered by the program you've developed?"

"Not at all. He seems to enjoy his time with me. Of course, he's never been a behavior problem. Just an underachiever. Now he's producing more and he's never complained."

"Jen, do you think that what you and the teachers are doing is helping Paul value learning? Do you think he's developing an increased love of reading? Has he really become a better student, or is he simply more compliant?"

Jen could feel herself becoming defensive as she talked with her colleague. "Well, I'm not sure if we're helping him develop a love for learning, but rewarding him has caused him to get more work done in school. Brenda, you're a classroom teacher. That's got to count for something, doesn't it?"

"Of course it does," she answered. "But what about the cost associated with the increased compliance Paul has given you?"

"Cost? What cost? You make it sound like there's a downside to a child doing more work in school!"

"Jen, you just said that you don't think this strategy is helping Paul develop a love of learning. I'd go further than that. I think what you're doing may decrease the chance of Paul discovering the true value and joy of learning. Why is Paul more productive now?"

"That's easy," Jen answered. "He works harder now so he can spend time with me in the gym or at the computer."

"Exactly, Jen. Paul is motivated by what he wants. He's internally motivated. He wants free time. He's working harder in school to earn the right to avoid academic work! With teacher approval! He's not motivated to learn more. As soon as you take away what he wants—the free time, the computer games—he'll revert to underachieving. The best you can hope for is that you haven't seriously compromised his capacity to care about working harder in school."

"The *best* I can hope for? What's that supposed to mean?" Jen was really angry now.

"Jen, I'm not questioning your intent. I know you want what is best for Paul. I'm just convinced that what you are doing is taking you further from *your* goal. Think about what Paul learns in a 'successful' incentive program: that working hard in school is only a means to an end. Learning is reduced to something done to get free time so he can go to the gym or play a computer game."

Brenda must have seen the look on her friend's face. "Jen, I'm not saying that you are *trying* to teach that to Paul. I'm only saying that's the message he almost assuredly gets. We learn so we can earn free time. Is that what you want to teach Paul?"

"Of course not. Is that what we're teaching him?" Jen had never really explored what a successful behavior mod program was teaching her students. Brenda was right: By rewarding kids, we teach them that learning has no intrinsic value. How many of us do it, unaware of the anti-educational message we're sending?

Brenda continued, "My favorite quotation about this is from *Punished by Rewards* by Alfie Kohn. He says, 'When you say *do this and you'll get that,* you devalue the *this.*' That's what we do to all the Pauls in our schools. When we say, 'Do your work and you get to play,' we're devaluing the work we ask kids to do. We affirm the notion that schoolwork is something we do so we can get the good stuff—like free time. If we hope to inspire kids academically and help them see the value and joy in learning, we've got to give up such self-defeating practices."

Brenda's comments made sense. Jen's incentive programs were not doing anything to help Paul become an inspired learner. While it was comforting to know that she was relying on old strategies because they represented what she knew and what she had thought was best for kids, Jen still had one problem: she didn't know what else to do! "You say Paul is internally motivated. That may be. All I know is that the only way I've been able to get him to buy into doing more schoolwork is by offering him free time in one form or another. Now you've got me thinking that's unhelpful at best and potentially harmful. What would you do with Paul? You're a classroom teacher. You must have encountered kids like Paul before."

"You're right, Jen. I am convinced that Paul is internally motivated. That doesn't mean he's motivated to do what *you* want him to do. It doesn't mean he's motivated to do *high-quality schoolwork.*" Brenda paused for a moment. "Remember, we can't *make* Paul or anyone else do anything. Still, I know what I would do with Paul. I'd begin by getting a clear picture of what *I* want. In order to be effective, I need to identify my role and my goal. I would want Paul to begin to value working harder in my class. Based on what you've told me, I'm seeing Paul as a student capable of doing competent work. Is that right? Is there a chance that he has an undiagnosed learning problem?"

"No," Jen replied. "We have had a number of discussions about Paul with our child study team. Everyone agrees that he is capable of doing grade-level work. His teacher sees it from time to time. His parents do as well. He shows no symptoms of a learning disability. He's just not motivated."

Brenda interrupted. "Your incentive program provides ample evidence that Paul is plenty motivated. When he sees something he wants, like a chance to get to the gym or a chance to play a game on the computer, he is willing to work hard. People who are willing to work hard to get what they want are certainly motivated."

"OK," Jen said. "Paul is motivated. How can we get him to be motivated to learn?"

Brenda smiled. "Wow! Seeing that internal motivation is present from birth is a major shift for you, Jen. So how do we get Paul motivated to value school? We've already seen the importance of avoiding any approach that devalues academic work, even unintentionally. So we know what *not* to do. We just need to decide what *to* do. Any ideas?"

"If I had any, I'm sure I would have tried them," Jen answered.

"More than anything else, it's crucial to help Paul appreciate *why* school is important and why the work he is asked to do is *relevant.* Do you think Paul has any idea why it is important to work hard and learn as much as possible?"

"I honestly don't know. I know that teachers feel increased pressure because of more and more high-stakes testing and increased curricular demands. You know that as well as anyone. They resent sacrificing any time to talk about *why* it's important to work hard in school. They believe that kids should trust them and do the work."

"I agree," said Brenda. "There's no doubt that the kids should trust us and do the work. Teachers shouldn't waste their time. One question: Is Paul the only kid in the class who isn't working to his potential?"

"Of course not," Jen said. "You know very well that far too many kids underachieve. That's probably the biggest complaint from teachers. Many students are fully capable but simply choose not to work very hard."

"So," Brenda continued, "would it be a *sacrifice* and a *waste of time* to explain to kids why learning is important? Right now, do enough kids 'trust them and work hard'? It seems to me that too many kids neither trust nor work hard. My emphasis is on helping kids like Paul discover the value in the work we ask them to do. Even if it takes time to do so, it is time well spent."

"Will it work?" Jen asked.

"I'm not sure," Brenda answered. "But if we don't change what we're doing, we'll never get different results. If we're not satisfied with how things are going, we've got to try something different. And unlike the dangers associated with an incentive program, this approach has no risk. Even if we're ineffective, we can't harm anyone."

"Do you think we can reach every kid?"

"Absolutely. If I didn't believe that, I'd quit teaching. I believe we *can* be successful with all students. First we need to develop a strong positive relationship with them. That's something you already do well, Jen. With that as a base, you've at least got a chance to help Paul build a picture of himself as a kid who values learning and being productive. He needs a picture of himself as a hard-working, successful student. Do you think he has that now?"

"Absolutely not," Jen replied. "He's a nice boy, but he's got no picture of himself as a successful student. How do I build that for him?"

"You can't," Brenda answered. "That's his job. Your job is to create the conditions that allow him to do that."

"So what do I do?"

"You've said that Paul occasionally works hard in school and does competent work. Is that right?"

"Yes," Jen replied. "It doesn't happen very often, but from time to time, Paul does some very good work, according to his teacher."

"It doesn't matter how often Paul does high-quality work, as long as he does it from time to time. What do you and the teacher typically do when Paul performs well?" Brenda asked.

"We praise him, of course," Jen answered. "We make a big deal about how proud we are of him."

"The next time Paul does well, don't praise him. Do something different, something that will connect to his sense of internal motivation," Brenda said.

"What are you suggesting?"

"Instead of praising Paul, ask him how he feels about being successful."

"But," Jen protested, "what if he doesn't feel good about doing well?"

"Jen, I'm convinced that Paul *does* feel good about his success. If it didn't feel good, he wouldn't ever work hard enough to achieve. Our feelings are the best indicator of how effectively we are satisfying our needs. When we are satisfying our needs, we feel good. I'm convinced Paul feels good when he is doing well in school."

"What happens next?" Jen asked.

"Assuming you have a strong relationship with Paul, which you do, he'll be willing to tell you that success in school feels good. That's the key right there, Jen. You can help Paul begin to see that he has control over how he feels by deciding how he acts in school. If he continues to act in ways that bring about school success, he'll feel good. That's the reward. The positive feeling that comes with success. Not time in the gym. Not playing a game on the computer. Feeling good about himself. Paul is old enough to understand that feeling good about yourself is worth working for. By focusing on the internal positive feelings instead of the external reward, you'll help Paul develop a picture of himself as a hard-working, productive student who wants to learn. Once that happens, Jen, you will have inspired a child. Nothing can be more satisfying to an educator than inspiring a kid."

The conversation ended. Jen was filled with a range of emotions, some of them conflicting. She was excited about working with Paul in a new way. She was eager to help him build a picture of himself as a hard-working, productive student. At the same time, she was nervous. Jen had been using an incentive program with Paul and he had begun to produce *some* work that the teacher found acceptable. Conflicted as she was, she decided to trust her instincts. Brenda was right. If Jen had been completely satisfied and comfortable with the behavior mod approach, she would have abandoned the ideas of internal motivation some time ago. It was clear she was intrigued. The time had come to discover if underachieving kids like Paul could be helped to develop pictures of themselves as hard-working, achieving students.

At first, Paul resisted. Even though he clearly liked discussing his success and how positive he felt about himself when he did well, Paul also liked the rewards he had been receiving. Jen was tempted to continue to give him external rewards while discussing his successes with him, but she stayed firm. Paul's resistance was short-lived. In fact, Paul liked discussing his good feelings more than playing on the computer or going to the gym. He loved discovering that he had control over his feelings by choosing to work hard on a regular basis. Within a couple of months, Paul had become a much more successful student. He still enjoyed regular contact with Jen, but he was maturing as a student. Talking about his successes and how he could maintain his positive feelings seemed to help Paul.

When Jen shared this success story with Brenda a few months later, Brenda appeared pleased. "Jen," she said, "it seems like you have created the classic 'win-win' situation. Paul is a happier, more successful student, one with a picture of doing well in school. You have succeeded with one more student. How do you feel?"

A wide grin spread across Jen's face. "Great!" she exclaimed.

Commentary

The apparent success of reward programs with young students is not at odds with internal control psychology. Elementary school students are frequently driven by the cooperative needs. Internally driven to seek approval and maintain positive connections, they naturally comply with the reward programs we create. Given the strong, positive relationship that exists between most elementary students and their teachers and an inherent drive to cooperate, young children typically behave in ways that result in "earning" rewards. They are not motivated by the external reward; they are driven by their internal desire to cooperate and maintain a positive relationship with a caring adult.

One unintended consequence of using a reward program with children is that it fosters an expectation that learning (an internal reward) is always accompanied by a tangible external reward, like free time or playing a game on the computer. Over time, students who have been externally rewarded often demand continued rewards to comply. Learning is no longer valued in its own right but is viewed simply as a way to earn an external reward.

Paul taught Jen a lot. Students who fall outside the norm always do when we pay attention. Whereas most of his 4th grade classmates were willing to work hard and perform for the tangible rewards being offered by his teachers, Paul was less driven by the cooperative needs and only complied when given something he valued (free time or playing a game on the computer). Jen discovered that Paul did not have an internal picture of himself as a hard-working, successful student. It is our internal pictures that motivate us. Without a strong desire to cooperate or succeed academically, Paul was destined to underachieve.

Paul needed to see the relevance of what he was being asked to do in order to become a successful student. When my daughter Melanie was in the 2nd grade, she put forth maximum effort "because Mrs. Watson said so!" Melanie's strong desire to cooperate and please was enough to drive her to achieve. The Pauls in our schools are different. They need to know the relevance of what they are doing before they will work hard. Once they understand why learning will add quality to their lives, these students almost always do well. Knowing the value of what they are asked to do allows them to create the internal motivation needed to do high-quality work. They move from minimal compliance based on external rewards to genuine quality based on the internal reward of learning.

Those who use external rewards are well-intentioned. They like kids and value learning. I do not question their commitment or intent. The problem with external rewards, as Jen discovered, is that they devalue learning. When students are told, "If you finish your work in the next 10 minutes, you can have five minutes to play a game," it devalues learning. Even though no educator means to send that message, it is delivered day after day in classrooms across the country.

Consider the difference between these two statements: "If you finish your work quickly, you can earn some free time" and "We have enough time to complete this assignment and still have a few minutes at the end of class for you to talk quietly with a classmate." The first statement casts learning as a burden that must be endured. The second offers the same opportunity to socialize without compromising the value of academics. There is nothing wrong with free time, a game on the computer, or a walk around the school. Good educators create an environment that allows students to meet the needs for freedom and fun because it supports learning. But even when we offer students some "down time," there is no need to simultaneously devalue the learning we cherish.

Jen discovered that even young students are motivated from the inside out. She helped Paul appreciate that learning feels good. By helping Paul build an internal picture of himself as a successful student, Jen facilitated his growth from minimal compliance to quality.

What You Can Do

• Remember that all students, even young ones, are motivated from the inside out.

• Help students build an internal picture of themselves as hard-working and successful.

• Help your students see the relevance of what they are asked to learn. When students ask you, "Why do we have to learn this?"—tell them! Their question is an opportunity to reveal the importance of what you are teaching.

• Become aware of the messages we send our students. When we offer them an external reward for academic achievement, we are sending an unintended message that demeans learning.

• Emphasize the positive feeling that accompanies high achievement. The reward for doing well is the good feeling a student experiences.

• Help students realize that they can feel good by behaving in ways that lead to academic success. Knowing you can succeed is need-satisfying and empowering!

Chapter 5

From Bossing to Leading

Some educators identify subtle changes they made after implementing strategies based on internal control psychology. While the results were significant, the shift was gentle. Not Jane. An elementary school principal, Jane characterized her shift as monumental. "Oh, yes," she told me. "Monumental is not too strong a word. I've heard stories about minor changes with major results. For me, the change was anything but subtle."

"Can you describe it for me, Jane?" I asked.

"Sure. The easiest thing is to contrast who I used to be with how I handle things today."

"OK. Start with the old Jane. Are you going to tell me you were unsuccessful as a principal?"

"That wasn't my plan," Jane answered with a laugh. "You won't see the changes I'm talking about in any performance evaluations or anything like that. I had been a principal in this district for six years before I became immersed in the ideas of internal control psychology. I had never given a lot of thought to my management style. In retrospect, I see that I was the poster child for boss management."

I'd known Jane for many years, and it was difficult to imagine her falling into the "boss manager" category. "Jane, with your easy manner and collaborative approach, it's hard to think of you as a boss manager. Tell me what you mean."

"I identify myself today as a 'recovering boss manager.' I used to be the caretaker for everybody in the school. I micromanaged everything. I had this insatiable need to be involved in every detail of the school. 'I don't like surprises,' was my mantra. I told the staff, 'Keep me informed. I'll handle it. That's what they pay me for.' I saw my job as being the problem solver so the teachers could put their energy into teaching. I figured if I ran the school smoothly, the teachers could concentrate on teaching, and we'd have a great school."

"Jane," I protested, "that doesn't sound especially bad. I know hundreds of teachers who would love to work for a principal who shouldered that responsibility and let them teach. Some would call that their dream principal."

"It's true that many teachers loved having a principal who took complete responsibility for the operation of the school. In fact, some teachers were uncomfortable when I decided to lead the staff rather than boss them. Lots of people love working for a kind, energetic, competent boss—a benevolent dictator. It's easier than working with a leader, because a collaborative approach requires more effort and input from staff. It may be more satisfying in the long run, but it's not an easy road, especially if a school has had a kind, effective boss running the show.

"You also said something about working 'for' a principal," Jane continued. "That word 'for' is important. In a traditional, boss-managed school, teachers work 'for' the principal. They may be lucky and work 'for' a competent boss. They may be less fortunate and have a less skilled boss. But in all cases, the teachers are working 'for' someone else." Jane paused. "In contrast, a lead management model invites the teachers to work 'with' the principal. It's a major shift in relationship. It's collaborative rather than hierarchical. It requires a lot more work and commitment on the part of the teachers. It's easier to work 'for' someone than to work 'with' someone. That's why lead management is so hard to implement effectively."

"It may be hard," I said, "but obviously you've done it. I'm interested in why you made the shift in the first place, and I'm interested in how you pulled it off, especially given how difficult it is."

"There were several things that led me to switch from bossing to leading. The first was becoming aware that I *was* a boss manager. Like I said, I had never given a lot of thought to my management style. I just knew that I ran an effective school, that the teachers liked and respected me, that teachers weren't asking to transfer to other buildings, and that the district office liked what was happening in our school."

"What helped you discover that you wanted to change, especially since you were already a successful administrator?"

Jane said, "I was in a workshop based on internal control and motivation, and we were discussing how we managed our schools. The participants were all administrators. During one of our sessions, it dawned on me that I was the focal point of everything that happened in my school. Everything ran through me. I was like this great mother goddess who took care of all her children. Looking back, it seems almost comical. At the time, however, it felt natural for me to be controlling everything."

"I'm still unclear about why you made the switch," I said.

"During the workshop, it struck me that I'm a person with a high need for power. I think most administrators have a high need for power. We learned in the workshop that all behavior is purposeful. I started thinking about how I managed my school, my teachers, and my students, trying to figure out the purpose behind my behavior. I discovered that having control down to the smallest detail was connected to my need for power. I want things done right, and I was convinced that if I was in the middle of every decision, things would be done right. My management style satisfied my need for power."

"How could you give up power," I asked, "if it's in your nature to seek power?"

"By relinquishing control," Jane answered, "I have even more power. Power is more than power *over* others. I'm not driven by a need to dominate; I'm driven to be competent. As I have become more of a leader, I'm a more competent administrator. As good as our school was before, it's better now. Staff attendance is better. Our kids do better on standardized tests. We have almost no vandalism. And people in the building smile more and enjoy their jobs more than they did in the past. There's less whining and complaining.

"Surrounded by that, my need for power is very well satisfied," said Jane. "I haven't given up a thing. I couldn't decide to 'need' less power. I'm internally driven to seek power and competence. What I could do, however, was adjust my picture of power as it related to being a school administrator."

"How did you do that?" I asked.

"That part was relatively easy," Jane replied. "I'm a logical, sequential thinker. I simply decided to become very clear about the kind of principal I wanted to be and set goals for myself. I embraced the notion that I have a high need for power and set about satisfying that need in ways that helped others become more competent and powerful at the same time. Let me give you an example. During my six years as building principal, I never had any teachers move into administration. I had a staff of competent teachers, but none of them ever moved on. In other schools across the district, a percentage of teachers moved from the classroom into administrative roles. I decided that my boss management style kept my staff from growing as much as they could. I decided I wanted to nurture their leadership potential rather than keep it under wraps.

"I also decided that I wanted to be more collaborative with the staff. There had always been a good-natured joke in our school that I practiced 'shared decision making'—'Jane makes all the decisions and shares them with us,' was the standard line. Like most jokes, there was an element of truth in what was being said. I decided that by intentionally practicing a more collaborative style, I would invite more energy and involvement from the teachers. The teachers were competent; I wanted to give them a chance to be more than that."

"How did you go about introducing 'the new Jane'? Were the teachers receptive, wary, confused?"

"At first," Jane began, "I didn't make any announcement. I started doing less 'for' the teachers so they could develop new areas of ability. Remember, my intent was completely positive. I was trying to give them more ownership in the school. I was acknowledging that they had areas of expertise that I didn't have. I thought they'd be delighted."

"Sounds like it wasn't that simple."

"Not at all. Initially, they thought I was getting lazy or tired or not feeling well. Since we had always worked well together as a staff, they let things slide for a while. After about a month, however, I heard about it. It was expressed as concern. Teachers wanted to know if I was OK. They told me I had been acting different, that I wasn't the Jane they were used to. I deflected their comments for a while, but then decided some explanation and dialogue were required. So I held a staff meeting.

"At the staff meeting, I told the teachers that I wanted to share power and make the school better by having more input from them. I told them they had areas of expertise that I didn't have, and I said that I thought we would be an even better school if I found ways to take advantage of their untapped potential."

"How did they take it?" I asked.

"If I was expecting the staff to celebrate, I was dead wrong. At first, they were quiet. Then I began to hear it. 'We're doing just fine,' they said. 'We don't need you to change. Things are going well. If it ain't broke, don't fix it.' These teachers had been benignly bossed for years. It was a very comfortable, symbiotic relationship. Just because I had decided to move forward, it didn't mean they were excited by the change.

"Even though no one said it, I think they were scared. We had a successful school. We had a certain way of doing things. I was shaking things up, and they were worried. I don't blame them. They might have thought this was a passing fad. This was out of character for me. I had taken them by surprise. I had always made only one significant demand: that they teach well. I had narrowly defined what they were required to do. They had no need to become more involved in any larger picture. As long as they took care of their piece, I made sure everything else got done and got done well."

"So what happened?"

"We muddled through," Jane said. "For the next month or two, no one really stepped forward and assumed a leadership role within the school. During this transition time, leadership was more a function of me not doing what I had always done. Once the teachers realized that I wasn't going to do everything 'for' them, they slowly began to do more."

"And what did you do?"

"I decided that the best thing for me to do, at least at first, was to do nothing. I simply watched and remained silent. I wanted to avoid praising them for their efforts. It seemed contrived and counter to what I was trying to foster. Me praising them for taking on more responsibility seemed like just another way to exercise 'power over' them, and that's not what I wanted. As a believer in the strength of internal motivation, I wanted the teachers to do what was meaningful and worthwhile for them. If they were motivated only by a desire to please me, they wouldn't put their hearts and souls into the tasks. Their halfhearted effort would only move us backwards. If this was to work, the staff had to be convinced that their increased involvement would be genuinely satisfying. They needed to be internally motivated.

"After a couple of months, we met as a staff. I then acknowledged those teachers who had assumed increased responsibility within the school. I asked them to evaluate how they felt when they stepped outside of the comfort zone we had collectively built over time. Because we had a good relationship, each of those teachers was able to admit to some fear and hesitation when they stretched themselves and ventured into new territory. More importantly, each was able to identify a level of excitement as they took on new tasks. A couple of teachers talked about how powerful it felt to expand their roles, regardless of how well things went.

"That was the beginning of us collectively turning the corner. After a few teachers took on more leadership responsibility within the school and identified how affirming it felt, the timid ones gave themselves permission to try as well. Within a few months, virtually all the teachers had somehow reinvented themselves. It wasn't that my authority was in any way diminished. I was still the building administrator, and only I had the authority to do certain things. I was still the official spokesperson for the building. But there was a profound change within the building.

"It was as if a sleeping giant had been awakened, and it was wonderful. I was always proud of our school. But when I was a controlling boss manager, we were limited by my ability. Once the entire staff became involved in the total life of the school, our horizons widened significantly. It was truly remarkable."

"So I guess it's fair to say that this has been successful for you," I said.

"Oh, yes," Jane said. "Very successful. It's interesting. In the few years that have passed since I switched to a more collaborative, lead management style, several of our teachers have moved on and become successful administrators themselves. I feel almost like a proud parent having given these teachers the opportunity to grow in ways that work for them. Others have stayed right here, but they will tell you that this place is an even better school today than it was a few years ago—and we were pretty good back then! The irony of this is how long it took me to figure it out."

"What do you mean?" I asked.

"We always tell teachers that one quality of a great teacher is to get the kids fully involved, not to do so much 'for' them, but to help them develop the competence to do for themselves. No one questions the wisdom of that approach. Still, when it comes to running a school—an analogous situation—most administrators limit what teachers do, do too much 'for' them, and unintentionally interfere with their ability to develop new competencies. If administrators behaved with our teachers the way we ask our teachers to behave with their students, we'd model effective leadership.

"I'm glad I learned about lead management and the importance of collaboration. It has helped our staff become more motivated from within, and the results are satisfying to all of us. I feel more successful than I have ever felt, and I know it's because I have found ways to tap into the creativity and energy of the staff. That energy and creativity were always there, but when I was a boss manager, I was limited by fear. I was afraid that if I gave power to the teachers, I would lose control of the school. Nothing could be further from the truth. As I relinquished control, the shared sense of ownership and responsibility helped us create a significantly better school. I would never go back to 'the good old days.' This is too much fun and too exciting."

Commentary

Jane's story is typical. Most administrators have a high need for power. The drive to achieve has motivated them to take on a leadership role. Because they want their school to be successful, many administrators behave like Jane, micromanaging everything and assuming complete control.

Controlling boss managers are generally well-meaning. As Jane discovered, however, their leadership style has a limiting effect on staff. More importantly, it has a limiting effect on the school. As long as Jane remained in the role of micromanager, her school was limited by what *she* knew and what *she* could do. When she allowed her staff to do more, her school had more participants in the leadership process. It became more vibrant and successful.

Jane learned that power is the drive to achieve and be competent. When she decided to foster a more collaborative approach, it did not diminish her power. Had it done so, Jane would not have persevered. As she tells us, she is driven to seek power. *How* she achieves power is up to her. Jane discovered that she achieved more power and felt more competent as an administrator as she became more collaborative and facilitated the professional growth of her staff.

Previously, Jane exercised "power over." Her "power over" orientation resulted in the staff becoming complacent and not developing their potential. By moving to a "power with" position, Jane enlisted the energy and wisdom of her staff. Teachers found new ways to grow and meet their own needs for power. Jane felt even more powerful. Most importantly, the school became even more effective.

Jane moved from bossing to leading, from micromanaging to collaborating. She learned there is more power in facilitation than there is in "power over." Jane reminds us that her situation is analogous to that of teacher and students. Within the classroom, teachers can become facilitators instead of micromanagers. They can help their students stretch and grow instead of doing too much for them. Teachers will achieve more power as they collaborate with their students in the pursuit of high-quality instruction.

What You Can Do

• Embrace your need for power. Power is the drive to achieve and be competent.

• Determine if you use "power over" behaviors with those you manage.

• Understand that a "power over" orientation is limited. Because of the inborn need for autonomy, those you manage will only tolerate so much before they undermine your authority.

• Develop collaborative skills. If you invite meaningful participation from those you manage, the school will reap the benefits of more minds, more creativity, more energy, more enthusiasm, and different points of view.

• Facilitate growth in others. The more power and competence you foster, the more you will have.

• Articulate the institutional goal and inspire those you manage to achieve objectives in multiple ways. Setting standards and giving freedom will result in higher quality.

Chapter 6

"Consequence" Is Not a Four-Letter Word

Nathan is a 4th grade student whose energy and enthusiasm would be problematic if he didn't have a skilled teacher who knows how to engage him and help him channel his boundless energy in an appropriate way. Because he has such a competent teacher, Nathan loves school and is experiencing both academic and social success.

I asked Nathan to tell me about his teacher. "My teacher teaches us a lot about choices in our class," Nathan began. "She tells us that even though we're just kids, we make choices all the time, like if we want to do our best in school. She talks about why we should try our best even with things that are kind of hard and boring. After those talks, I know that school is my job and I want to do my best. She's real nice, probably the best teacher I've ever had in my whole life. I like her a lot!"

"What makes your teacher so good?" I asked.

"She makes school fun. Sometimes we do things that are a little bit boring, but mostly our class is fun. Some of my friends have teachers who aren't so nice and who don't make class this much fun, and they don't like school so much. I love school and think I always will if I keep having teachers like the one I have now."

"Nathan," I said, "can you tell me exactly what your teacher does to make school so much fun for you?"

"One thing is that we do lots of projects. In my old school, we used to do lots of worksheets and fill in the blanks. In this school, we don't do hardly any worksheets. Projects are better because they are more interesting. Our teacher tells us that when we are working on a project we're really doing two or three things at the same time. We just finished this science project about habitats, but it was also an English language arts project because we had to write a story. And it was also an art project because we had to do a display. So doing one project was like doing all three subjects at the same time. I like that and so do my friends."

"What else do you like about your class?"

"I like that we work in groups a lot. Sometimes we don't, and when we have tests we usually work by ourselves, but most of the time we work with other kids. My teacher changes the groups a lot so we work with different kids. At first I didn't like that so much because I liked being with my old friends. But the teacher says it's good to learn to work with different people, so she always changes the groups. Once I got used to that I liked it even better, because when you work with more kids you make more friends. Now I have more friends in my class than I did when the school year started."

"Nathan, you told me that your teacher talks about choices. Tell me more about that."

"When she gives us work to do, she tells us two or three ways we can do it. Like when we were doing a book report, one time she told us we could read any book we wanted as long as it was about a person. Another time, she told us we could write a report or do a poster and tell the class about the book. I like it when we have choices. She also talks about consequences."

"That sounds interesting," I said. "What does she tell you about consequences?"

"Most kids think that consequences are bad, but our teacher says that consequences can be good, too. If you do your work and pay attention in class, you'll probably do good on a test. That's a consequence. I used to not like consequences because I thought they were bad. Now I like them because I know I can make choices that will have a good consequence."

"Is there anything else you want to tell me about your class?"

"The last thing I mostly like about my class is that my teacher is really nice. She hardly ever yells at us and is never in a really grumpy mood. All the kids want to be good for her because she's so nice. Some teachers think they're nice because they give you things like pizza parties. Our teacher never gives us those things. She's just nice to us all the time and you can tell she really likes kids. In a class like mine, it's easy to have fun and learn lots of interesting things like we did about the habitats. I hope all teachers will be as good as the one I have this year."

Commentary

Elementary school children tell us about good teaching when we take time to listen. All else being equal, Nathan has a good chance of being a successful student because he loves school. One primary responsibility of elementary school teachers is to inspire kids to love school and love learning.

Nathan said he especially enjoys school because it is "fun." Many elementary school students, including Nathan, are driven by the cooperative needs of belonging and fun. Nathan specifically mentioned that he enjoys the group work his teacher provides, something that allows him to connect while being academically productive. Nathan's teacher frequently mixes up the group configuration to foster a sense of community. Creating a classroom that supports the drives for fun and belonging inspires students to engage in high-level academic work.

Nathan's teacher has helped students realize that consequences can be either positive or negative. Most elementary school kids will tell you that consequences are "bad." It's helpful for kids to learn that consequences can be positive. The consequence of studying for a test is that you will learn more and probably earn a higher grade. The consequence of doing your homework is that you are prepared for class and able to positively participate. When students learn that consequences can be positive and that they flow naturally from the choices they make, they feel an increased sense of control.

When we listen to elementary school students, they tell us how to create classrooms that inspire the highest-quality learning. Nathan points us in the right direction.

What You Can Do

• Create classrooms that support the need for fun. Elementary school teachers inspire students when they create a love of learning. A joyous atmosphere is essential.

• Provide opportunities for students to work in groups. It supports the need for belonging.

• Change groups regularly to build community and break down barriers within a classroom.

• Teach students that "consequence" is not a four-letter word. Teach them that consequences can be positive and that they can choose behaviors that will have positive consequences.

• Help students develop a work ethic by emphasizing that their "job" in school is to work hard and learn as much as possible. Students who embrace that role will learn more than students who adopt a more passive orientation toward school.

Part III

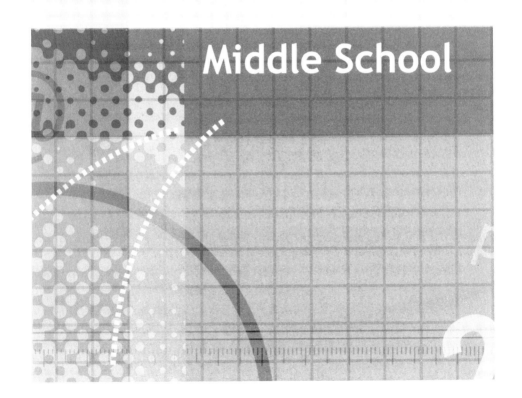

Middle School

Chapter 7

Positive Relationships Support Competence and High Standards

A middle school social studies teacher, Linda found her curriculum incredibly full. She had always wished it were scaled back so she taught fewer concepts but in greater depth. In the past couple of years, Linda has derived more satisfaction from her job. She is quick to mention that her new approach is no easier. In fact, it may be harder. But she's learned that "teaching happier" is more important than "teaching easier."

It started when Linda's district began to look at standards-based education (SBE). While Linda does not claim to be an expert in SBE, moving to that technique helped her organize her teaching. In SBE, concepts are identified as "essential to know," "important to know," and "nice to know," typically depicted as three concentric circles, with "essential to know" being the center, or bull's-eye.

Linda identifies the social studies curriculum in grade 8—U.S. History—as "massive." She always felt overwhelmed. Complicating matters was her method of grading. Like many secondary school teachers, Linda used a "point system." Students earned points in everything from class participation, to homework, to tests and quizzes, to projects. At the end of the term, Linda would calculate the percentage of points the kids had earned and issue grades accordingly. She wanted to be flexible, so she offered kids opportunities to do additional work—she hated calling it "extra credit."

By immersing themselves in something they enjoyed, kids could earn points and improve their grades.

As a result, Linda's grades were "fair" but communicated little to students and parents about what had been learned. Two students could earn a *B* in Linda's class yet have done very different things to achieve their grades. All a *B* meant was that the student had earned between 80 and 89 percent of the total points for "required" work. Even that is not completely accurate. Some kids earned less than 80 percent of the "required" points, but got a legitimate *B* because of the additional work they had chosen to do.

SBE helped the social studies department become better organized as a whole. The teachers collectively decided to use the state standards as guides. Using the curriculum frameworks, they created an agreed-upon cluster of concepts that were essential to know, important to know, and nice to know at each grade level. This gave their teaching more focus and provided a reasonable chance of teachers receiving and passing on students who had substantial commonality in what they knew and were able to do, so teachers could teach more effectively.

The SBE approach affected Linda's teaching dramatically. Rather than feeling overwhelmed, she had direction about where to put her emphasis. Admittedly, there was less freedom for the students in terms of "additional" work they could do, but there was enough flexibility that no learner was boxed in.

Despite her enthusiasm for SBE, Linda was still uncomfortable. There seemed to be a disconnect between her grading system and the departmental stance that some things were essential to know. Put simply, even though some kids didn't master everything identified as essential to know, they moved on because they had amassed enough points. The teachers who received Linda's former students got more consistency, but there was still more variability than she liked.

About that time Linda heard about a workshop called "The Competence-Based Classroom." She wasn't sure what it was, but the title got her attention and she decided to attend. She was not disappointed.

After attending this training, Linda came to the conclusion that the Competence-Based Classroom (CBC) was what she needed to make her SBE approach more effective. Based on the work of William Glasser, the CBC grew out of the realization that too many kids were leaving school without being competent. A primary culprit is our current grading practice. In most traditional schools, students can do *D* work, identified as "poor" or "below average," and still move on. They may be denied admission to the next level of a foreign language or more advanced math, but they can earn promotion and graduate from high school without ever doing competent work!

In a CBC, the only grades a student can earn are *A* (for truly superior work, above and beyond our expectations), *B* (for competent work that matches our expectations for students), or "Incomplete" (or some grade that communicates that the student has not yet completed the course because they haven't yet demonstrated competence). The CBC completely closes the loophole that results in kids doing substandard work but moving through our system right through graduation.

It was relatively late in the school year when Linda learned about the CBC. It seemed wonderful in the workshop, but Linda had seen lots of things that looked great in a workshop and were disappointing when put into practice. She was hoping the CBC wasn't one of them.

When the next unit was about to begin, Linda held a class meeting. Class meetings are common in classrooms that apply the principles of internal control psychology. Kids feel connected. Because they can "pass" if they do not wish to actively participate, it meets the need for freedom. The democratic nature of a class meeting helps kids feel listened to, increasing their sense of power in the classroom. Finally, most students report that class meetings are fun, especially when they are used regularly and not just when there is a problem to discuss.

Linda began by telling the class, "I'd like to organize things differently for our next unit. We've been looking at our circles before each unit so you know what's 'essential to know.' We're still going to use our circles, but I'd like to add something to it.

In fact, because everyone will earn an *A* or a *B,* I'm hoping you'll be as excited as I am. Does the idea of knowing that you'll get an *A* or a *B* seem like a good one?"

Her grade 8 students were interested and curious. And they all liked the idea of getting at least a *B.* They were skeptical, but ready to hear how this was going to work.

"We'll use our circles, and if you master everything within the 'essential to know' area, you will earn a *B.* I'll give you all the details about what you have to know and how you can demonstrate your learning to me as we go along. At this point, all you need to remember is that completing the 'essential' area results in a *B.*"

"How do we get an *A*?" someone asked.

"There are two ways to get an *A,*" Linda answered. "You can complete all of the 'essential' elements plus some of the 'important' and 'nice to know' parts. We'll discuss the specifics as we work through this. We'll figure it out together and you'll know exactly what the requirements are ahead of time. No surprises. Promise." By telling the kids that they would "figure it out together," she was giving them a way to achieve power by being actively involved in the academic and evaluative process. This engaged her students and inspired them to work harder because she was making them partners in their own education.

"What's the other way?" a student asked.

"If you have completed everything in the 'essential' area, you can help another student who hasn't yet mastered that material. Working as a kind of teacher assistant will be another way to earn an *A.*"

One student immediately said, "My parents will never allow that. They think that teaching is *your* job. I'm here to learn, they always tell me. If they found out you were making me teach someone else, they'd be insanely angry."

"I'm glad you brought that up. I'll send a notice to your parents so that they know what's going on. In it, I'll tell them that people learn a tremendous amount when they teach something to another person. If your parents don't realize that, I can understand why they would be upset if you were teaching a classmate.

Once they realize that you *are* learning as you help a classmate, they may actually like the idea. Even if they don't, no one will be *required* to do this. If you or your parents would rather you not function as a teacher assistant, you can still earn an *A* by extending your learning beyond the 'essential' circle."

Linda knew the next question would come. She just wasn't sure who would ask it.

"Suppose I just want a *C*?" The question came from Josh, a student who didn't seem to care much about how well he did and didn't seem to have a lot of support from his parents regarding schoolwork.

"At this point," Linda explained, "the only grades on the menu are *A* and *B*. I wouldn't be doing my job and you wouldn't be doing yours if I accepted anything less than what we identify as 'essential.' If you don't learn the material, it will be difficult for you in the future. Since my goal is to help you develop the skills you'll need to be successful in high school, I will do everything I can to help you have the strongest possible foundation. So what do you think?"

Kara raised her hand. "I guess I like the idea OK. I think everyone would be happy knowing they'll get an *A* or *B*. I'm just a little confused. What will you do about kids who don't do what they're supposed to do?"

"Right now, my plan is to issue no grade," Linda replied.

"What do you mean?" several students asked in unison.

"Just that. No grade. Instead of giving you a poor grade for not doing what is 'essential,' I'll leave your report card blank. If you receive a *D,* you pass, even though you haven't shown me that you've got the skills we think you need. Even if you fail, most kids go to summer school and get promoted to the next grade anyway. I'll just leave the report card blank until you show me you know what you need to know and can do what you need to do."

"What will the parents think?" one student asked.

"If I explain the process well enough ahead of time, parents will know what a blank grade means. If not, I'm hoping they'll get in touch with me. I believe your parents want you to leave this class equipped with the skills and knowledge you'll need to be successful in high school."

This seemed to satisfy the students, and Linda and her students began their Competency-Based Classroom experiment with excitement. Taking time to talk about this with her students in a class meeting before implementing it was crucial because it helped them develop a shared vision of what they wanted. Knowing that kids are internally motivated, Linda needed the kids to buy into the concept before forging ahead.

That first unit was almost like a miracle. Every one of Linda's students demonstrated they knew what was identified as "essential to know." About 40 percent went above and beyond in some way and earned an *A*. Some worked as assistants to others in the class. Some completed additional work to move their grades from a *B* to an *A*. No one tested her by doing less. Linda was certain that more students did better work during that unit than any other unit she had ever taught. It was exciting. That year ended on a high note, and Linda was committed to fully implementing the CBC the following school year.

•   •   •

When she returned to school after the summer, Linda held a class meeting and explained the CBC to her new students with energy and excitement. When they first heard about it, the students seemed genuinely excited about having a classroom where their success was all but guaranteed. Again, Linda was intentionally nurturing the kind of internal motivation that was needed for this to work. Despite the initial enthusiasm, however, problems soon emerged. Many middle school students aren't especially organized. By the time they have reached the 8th grade, some have identified themselves as poor students and have become comfortable doing mediocre work. Furthermore, middle school kids are present tense–oriented. The idea of receiving no grade at the end of the marking period doesn't mean much to them at midterm. It's too far away to be relevant to many of them.

Trust is an important value to middle school kids. When Linda told them at the beginning of the year that they would receive only an *A*, a *B*, or no grade, some needed to find out if Linda was telling the truth or just trying to "trick" them into working harder. Her students—lots of them—were testing her. They figured if enough of them didn't do competent work, Linda would revert to giving the *C* and *D* grades so many of them had come to expect.

At the end of the first marking period, about half of Linda's students received no grade in social studies. Many were genuinely surprised when they received their report cards. "What are we supposed to do now?" they asked.

"You still need to do the essential work and earn the *A* or *B* I know you can earn. We still have time. The grade can be changed. You have some catching up to do, but I'm confident you can do it."

"Suppose we don't?" someone asked.

"Then you'll have no grade for the whole year," Linda answered.

"So we'll have to go to summer school?"

"I'm not sure. Summer school is for kids who fail during the year. You haven't failed. You just haven't earned a grade. I'm not sure what will happen. It's only November, and school doesn't get out until June. I haven't thought that far ahead. I'd rather you do the work." Linda tried to use a nonjudgmental tone. At the same time, she was pleased that some kids saw that their choices had consequences.

"Could we have to repeat the grade?"

"I really don't know. I guess it's possible. But you're spending your energy on something that doesn't have to be a problem. All you have to do is complete your work, and you'll be all set." Linda was trying to remain positive with these students, but she was not upset that many of them were becoming uncomfortable. She was letting them take responsibility and figure out how to remedy the situation they had created.

Throughout the year, things improved slowly but steadily. The number of blank grades decreased each term. During the final quarter, Linda still had students completing work from the first half of the year, but at least she knew that they had learned the essentials of each unit.

Near the end of the school year, only a handful of kids had blank grades. Linda and the principal met with the students and gave each of them a complete list of what they needed to do to earn a *B*. They were told that they would need to attend summer school if they didn't successfully complete the work by the deadline. Of the seven kids in that group, three didn't do the work and were given failing grades for the year.

At first, Linda felt like a failure. She had visions of every student doing *B* or *A* work. She had never worked so hard as a teacher. When Linda had implemented the CBC the year before for one unit, it was easy, exciting, and successful. Applying it all year was a different story. The greatest challenge (and headache) was the record keeping and paperwork. In May and June, kids were working on assignments that were begun in September and October. Kids knew that as long as they got the work done and *eventually* demonstrated competence, they would earn a *B*.

In reviewing this yearlong effort, she identified several major flaws. One related to the concepts of work ethic and responsibility. As a teacher, Linda believes she is doing more than teaching content to students. She is helping them develop habits that will serve them well in school and beyond. Many kids don't have a strong work ethic and haven't learned how to act responsibly as students. By allowing kids to turn in work months after it was assigned, she may have unconsciously contributed to a poor work ethic. Developmentally, middle school kids needed more structure. By giving them more freedom than they could responsibly handle, Linda helped them dig some pretty big academic holes. Even though all but three managed to successfully dig themselves out, it didn't need to be so difficult.

Record keeping was incredibly time-consuming. Linda didn't mind spending time outside of school to be a great teacher, but she wanted to spend as little as possible on clerical tasks. She needed to streamline the process.

Finally, Linda was concerned about how others perceived the CBC. Colleagues and parents saw it as "soft" or "easy." Paradoxically, Linda was drawn to the CBC because it requires all students to demonstrate competence. It is demanding. Still, if both colleagues and parents perceived it as less rigorous, Linda needed to implement it more effectively.

As the school year ended, Linda needed to decide if she was going to use the CBC again or return to a more traditional approach. In her district, teachers are given enough academic freedom that the decision was hers to make. Linda had a conversation with her principal to figure out what she wanted. He had been supportive of her efforts, and she valued his opinion.

John got Linda thinking by asking, "As a teacher, Linda, what do you most want?"

"My goal is for the kids to learn as much as possible," she replied. Linda had given a lot of thought to how her thinking had evolved over the years. When she began her career, she focused on "covering" the material. She then put more emphasis on "teaching" the material, even if she covered less. Recently, Linda had shifted the focus from her ("teaching") to the students ("learning").

"OK," John said. "Begin there. This year, you used a different process in teaching and assessing kids. Do you think the kids learned less, more, or about the same as your students in past years?"

This question cut through Linda's conflicted feelings and got to the heart of the matter. The answer was remarkably easy. "I have no doubt that my students learned more this year than in any other year I have taught. As difficult as this year was, I am certain that the kids did higher-quality work."

"What's the problem, then?" John asked, with that familiar smile on his face and twinkle in his eye.

"As unprofessional as it sounds," Linda admitted, "it was way too much work."

"So we've moved from a huge philosophical problem to how to implement the CBC more efficiently. Is that it?"

"Mostly," Linda said, "although there is still one philosophical part. But it's mostly about how to implement it without driving myself crazy."

"Let me ask you another question before we go on," John said. "Can you envision going back to the way you used to teach and assess?"

"Absolutely not!" Linda was amazed by how quickly and energetically she answered.

"Then you need to figure out how you can do it more efficiently, without burning yourself out."

"You're right," Linda said. "Now that we're talking about it, I realize I could never go back to routinely giving out *C*s, *D*s, and *F*s. I feel so much better about myself as a teacher using the CBC. I just need to figure out how to do it better. And easier."

"You did say you had one philosophical dilemma as well," John reminded her.

"Yes," Linda replied. "It's the whole work ethic/responsibility thing. I'm afraid that by having no firm deadlines, I'm letting kids think that they can do things on their own schedule and not act responsibly. Adolescents are egocentric enough. They don't need me to feed their self-centeredness."

The conversation ended with Linda having a renewed commitment to the CBC, with some revisions concerning implementation. The following year, she instituted a few changes that made things easier, supported the work ethic she values, and maintained the higher-quality academic work she had seen the year before. The change that seemed to make all the difference was adding the grade of *C* for those students who turned in their work late. Linda told the students, "You will be responsible for demonstrating competence on everything that is identified as 'essential to know.' If you get it done in a timely way, you will earn an *A* or *B*. If you are late with your work, you'll receive a *C* for the same work. I hope you choose to turn your work in on time since you're going to do it regardless."

For the most part, Linda took a low-key approach to this change. She decided that having a more casual, matter-of-fact tone would be more effective with middle school kids than giving them a heavy-handed lecture. The one thing she did emphasize was the fact that she had a life outside of school and that turning in work on time was a sign of respect.

Her second full year of running the CBC was a huge success for Linda. Kids continued to do higher-quality work, and the insistence on promptness helped them overcome their adolescent tendency to procrastinate. Linda's class had earned the reputation as one in which "you'll get a good grade but you'll have to earn it." That's the kind of reputation she wanted! Running a CBC has helped Linda become more like the teacher she has always wanted to be.

Commentary

Linda did her best to issue grades that were fair and meaningful. Using a point system like many secondary school teachers, Linda's grades were "fair." What troubled Linda—and what troubles many teachers—is that even "fair" grades do not necessarily communicate what students have learned. Students, parents, and future teachers cannot tell what has been learned by looking at the grade.

Linda's story highlights two important initiatives: standards-based education and the Competence-Based Classroom. Both models have merit, but neither can stand alone successfully. SBE provides clarity about *what* to teach and what to emphasize. It does not guarantee that students will *learn* what is being taught. The CBC offers a model of *how* to teach, but it provides no specifics about the content. Students can regularly do competent work and still not master what is essential. Linda blended SBE and the CBC, addressing both the *what* and the *how* that make up effective teaching.

Standards-based education helped Linda and her department develop consistency in what was taught. By agreeing upon what was essential to know, important to know, and nice to know, teachers focused their energy more effectively. Teachers sacrificed some autonomy and gave up some "favorite" topics, but they did so because they collectively determined what elements fit into which category. SBE ensured the consistency necessary for organizational success.

The specifics provided by SBE support the effectiveness of the CBC. The CBC assures students of achieving power (competence) as long as they work hard. Students are motivated when they perceive success as attainable. With teacher instruction and peer support, all students can achieve in the CBC. Addressing the need for power/competence is not sufficient, however. The CBC would have been far less effective if Linda had not fostered positive relationships with her students. Through the use of class meetings, she engaged students and made them partners in the creation and implementation of the CBC. Without a strong relationship, many students would choose not to put forth their best effort, but Linda engaged her students, helping them be successful.

Setting standards is all well and good, but standards are meaningless unless students work to achieve them. At the same time, having students demonstrate competence does not mean they are mastering what is essential. Linda put together standards-based education and the Competence-Based Classroom to create a classroom where students mastered what is essential. Her grades not only reflected that her students had performed well, they communicated to all interested parties precisely what had been learned.

What You Can Do

• Develop positive relationships with students. You need students to be engaged if you expect them to do high-quality work.

• Regularly conduct class meetings with your students. Such meetings are need-satisfying, engage students in the educational process, and lead to greater student achievement.

• Get a clear picture of what you want your students to know and be able to do. Standards-based education provides one effective process to help teachers prioritize what is to be taught.

• Communicate to students that you expect them to be competent and that you have confidence in their ability to succeed.

The CBC addresses the needs for power/competence, increasing the chances that students will put forth the effort needed to be successful in a rigorous academic environment.

• Be prepared for students to test you. Students who have not demonstrated competence in the past will often settle for barely passing grades. They need your support. You must remain resolute in order to help these students become successful. More than anything else, a positive relationship is needed with reluctant learners who are accustomed to school failure.

Chapter 8

Self-Evaluation Leads to Lasting Change

The last two years have been a whirlwind for Ben. He's been a middle school counselor for almost 15 years. Ben enjoys a good reputation among his peers and within the community, in part because he's known as someone who "gets things done" and has a lot of success with kids.

When the head of guidance in Ben's district said he was scheduling a workshop about internal control psychology, Ben was one of the more vocal skeptics. Ben was well-versed in stimulus-response psychology and had success using behavior modification with middle school kids. Even though he didn't know a lot about psychologies based on internal motivation, Ben knew he would be going to the workshop with some negativity.

Ben was told that internal control psychology takes the position that people are internally motivated. Ben knew from years of experience that external motivators like the fear of a serious grounding or the enticement of a healthy monetary reward for good grades had saved a lot of middle school kids from failure, at least while they were under his care. Ben had heard that practitioners of internal control psychology typically placed an emphasis on building relationships. While he didn't have an argument with that, he didn't think it took into account what happens in a typical school. School counselors have heavy caseloads. Ben believed he needed to move kids in and out quickly so he could put out the next fire. What he had heard about internal control psychology sounded time-intensive and unwieldy in a school setting.

On the third day of the workshop, participants broke into groups and talked about the strength of the needs that drive human behavior. Ben said he thought his strongest needs were for freedom and fun. "That's interesting, Ben," said Erica. "I wouldn't have guessed those to be your strongest needs. Tell us more."

"Sure," Ben said. "Freedom is the most obvious. I think it's why I went into education and specifically into counseling. I have a lot of pride in what I do, but I'm not ashamed to say that I love my time off. And as much as I liked being a classroom teacher, I have more freedom as a counselor. I can remember lots of days when I'd really be into something exciting with the students in my history class and we'd have to stop because the bell rang. As a counselor, even though I'm always putting out fires and running, I set my own schedule and am not restricted by bells."

"What you say, Ben, is true for a lot of educators," said Erika. "What about the fun need?"

"I see myself as someone who seeks to create enjoyment in everything I do. My approach has always been, 'If it's worth doing, then it's worth enjoying.' I guess that links up with belonging. As a counselor, I see myself as a people person, so I'd put the need for belonging up there as well."

Another member of the group, Pete, chimed in, "The only two you haven't mentioned, Ben, are survival and power."

"Well," Ben said, "survival simply isn't something I spend a lot of energy thinking about. I'm not an exercise fanatic. I stay in reasonably good shape, but I'm not extreme about what I eat. I don't spend a lot of time thinking about security issues and saving for the future."

"OK," said Pete. "But what about power? Certainly you've got a pretty big power need, wouldn't you agree?" Ben laughs about it now. He readily acknowledges that he has a high need for power. But at that moment, he was both angered and dumbfounded—angered that his colleagues saw him as a "power freak," and dumbfounded that anyone could see a counselor as someone with a high need for power. "Are you guys saying I'm some type of power freak?" Ben asked. Actually, it was more of an accusation than a question. Fortunately, Erica, Pete, and Ben had worked together for several years and had a strong working relationship that could withstand such conversations.

"Ben," Erica began, "no one is calling you a power freak. I do see you as someone with a high need for power, but I don't mean that in a 'power over' way. I don't see it as a negative at all. You know you're a good counselor, right?"

"Sure. Being good at my job is important to me."

"I think that's what we were both thinking," said Pete. "Sure, you're a guy who likes to have fun, but you're all about the work. You take your job and yourself seriously—in a good way. You really want to make a difference in the lives of kids, and you've worked hard to develop your reputation as a good counselor. That's power, Ben."

"Well," Ben said, the defensiveness all but gone, "put that way, I guess I do have a strong need for power. I don't think I could stomach being a mediocre counselor. It's important that I succeed at what I do. If that's what we mean by power, then I definitely see myself as having a big power need."

Ben began to make the switch from seeing things externally to seeing things internally. The external orientation meant Ben concentrated on what his job did *for others.* He made kids more successful in school. They were empowered by what he did. He looked at *them* when thinking about his job. Suddenly, Ben started looking at *himself* when he thought about his job—not in an egocentric or negative way, but in a way that allowed him to see what being successful meant for *him,* not just for the kids.

Since then, Ben has made more discoveries that have changed the way he approaches his job and conceptualizes what it means to be a counselor. The internal motivation workshop took place early in the summer. Ben spent the rest of the summer on vacation, affirming that his need for freedom was as important as he had thought. When school began, Ben fell quickly into the rhythm that had become comfortably familiar after 15 years. He was still committed to the tried-and-true behavior modification programs he had used so successfully. He was still overworked, and he puzzled about how spending too-scarce time developing relationships was going to help him do his job better. In fact, now that he knew success on the job was linked to his need for power, Ben was convinced that he was using the most effective behaviors available.

Everything was going along fine until there was a departmental meeting between the middle school counselors and the high school counselors. There had never really been any give-and-take among counselors from the different levels before, but at this meeting the topic was a discussion of the freshman class and how well they were doing a few months into the school year.

Recalling that meeting, Ben says, "I'd just never thought very much about my counselees after they left the middle school because I was focused on my new caseload. Names were brought up, and our high school colleagues talked about which kids were doing especially well, which ones seemed to have settled in nicely at the high school, and which ones were academic train wrecks. It seems that all my brilliant counseling at the middle school level was an illusion. Some of the kids who were failing miserably were the same ones I had allegedly 'fixed' with rewards and incentives during those formative middle school years."

In retrospect, Ben believes that he was an unintentional coconspirator. Ben created the behavior modification programs to get kids to work harder in school, to avoid retention or summer school, or to earn something special from Mom and Dad. The kids didn't particularly care about the schoolwork Ben was promoting. They just wanted to avoid additional school in the form of summer school or grade retention. Or they were motivated by that "special something" promised from home. So they complied. The teachers had more compliant students who produced more work. ("It's funny," Ben said to me. "I never remember us having much conversation about the kids learning more. We focused on the fact that there were more check marks in the gradebook and more assignments turned in on time.") The teachers were happy and appreciated all Ben had done to "make the kids work harder." Because "making the kids do better" helped Ben feel competent, he felt good about himself and believed he was helping kids develop a sense of responsibility.

There was only one problem: It wasn't true. Kids left the middle school with no greater love for learning and no greater appreciation for the value of a good education. They had not developed a genuine sense of responsibility. Once they got to the high school, they immediately reverted to their old, unproductive ways. Ben's work hadn't led to any substantive change. If anything, it had made things worse, because now the kids essentially demanded to be "paid off" for doing even minimally competent work. "Why should I do it if you won't give me blah, blah, blah?" they demanded. They had never been given any reason to work hard other than avoiding summer school, avoiding retention, or getting some tangible reward.

As a result of the meeting, Ben remembered something mentioned in the summer workshop: Perceptions are based, in part, upon knowledge. Ben had just been given unpleasant new knowledge, and he no longer perceived himself as the competent, successful counselor he wanted to be.

It was at this moment that Ben truly understood what having "out-of-balance scales" meant. There was a huge difference between the internal picture he had of himself as a counselor and his new perception of the counselor he really was. Interestingly, no one else viewed Ben differently. He was just as respected by his colleagues as he had always been. The difference was all internal, but it had a profound effect on Ben.

Ben now saw himself as a counselor with a need for power who was feeling powerless and ineffective. Since being competent at work was important to Ben, he decided to take action. It wasn't enough that those around him continued to hold him in high regard. Unless he changed, Ben would no longer hold himself in high regard. That was a price he was unwilling to pay.

Fortunately, Ben remembered discussions about the difference between the unique internal pictures we create and the basic needs that we all share. What Ben determined was that getting kids to do what he thought was right for them was his way to get power. Although he had not realized it at the time, it was a "power over" orientation. Ben set himself up as the expert and implemented an incentive-threat program. Since the kids generally complied, at least to some extent, Ben felt powerful.

As Ben examined things from an internal control perspective, he decided that he didn't like getting power by having power over others and getting them to do what he thought they should do. Ben wanted to achieve "power with" by helping kids discover that working hard in school and learning as much as possible would enhance their lives.

Also, Ben had learned that his "power over" strategies had produced only short-term gains. Once out of his sphere of influence and without the external rewards and threats he systematically kept in front of them, Ben's former counselees slipped back into well-known habits of underachievement. Ben acknowledged that he was not being successful, at least not over time. It was this recognition that helped Ben become a more successful counselor.

Ben recalled learning that what we want is subject to change. He was genetically instructed to seek power, but Ben had options about the pictures he created to satisfy that need. Until then, most of his power pictures were "power over, let me control you, I know what's best for you, just leave it to me" pictures. Ben decided to create new pictures. Never had Ben been so intentional about creating a picture of what he wanted as a counselor. This conscious reflection was a difficult but fruitful process. Ben decided that he would judge his success on what *he* did, not on what the kids did as a result of his interventions. He decided to take ownership of his behavior and take responsibility for what he did. At the same time, Ben would not give over power to another by evaluating himself on what *others* chose to do. Ben would be responsible for his decisions and his actions, and others would be responsible for theirs.

Ben decided to focus his energy on helping kids develop responsibility and become good decision makers in the long run. Historically, Ben had always been someone who looked at immediate results: the next homework assignment, the next project, the next quiz. While these issues continued to matter, Ben decided they didn't matter *more than* helping kids learn things that would be helpful to them over time.

A kid choosing not to do his or her best work on the next project wasn't *Ben's failure*. Instead, he saw it as *the student's choice;* Ben's job was to figure out how to help the student learn as much as possible from his or her decisions. Previously, when kids did well, Ben lavishly praised them and told them how much closer they were to achieving their goals (avoiding summer school, getting that prized external reward, etc.). Conversely, when students failed to do what they were supposed to do in school, Ben kindly but firmly told them how they had made poor choices and told them the consequences, making sure they understood how bad those consequences were.

Now, Ben asked lots of self-evaluation questions instead of dispensing rewards and sanctions: "How did that go for you? Are you pleased with how this is going?" One of Ben's new strategies was intentionally removing parents from his conversations with kids. Previously, Ben would often ask questions like, "Do you want your parents to be proud of you? Do you think they'll be happy when they see this test/project/report card?" Although he hadn't realized it at the time, Ben was perpetuating an external orientation by routinely referencing parental expectations.

Now he took the parents out of his discussions with kids. From a developmental perspective, young adolescents are try-ing to separate themselves from their parents and create their own identities. From an internal motivation perspective, Ben had learned that adolescents typically have an especially strong need for freedom. Focusing on the student without reference to parental authority was aligned with the adolescent need to be autonomous.

Ben's questioning now sounded more like this: "So, are you pleased with how you did on this assignment?" He was amazed how many kids would allude to their parents as they answered. ("My parents are going to be so disappointed in me. They'll prob-ably ground me for life!") To help kids move from an external orientation of pleasing or disappointing another, Ben now said,

"I want you to forget about your parents for a minute. I want you to think about exactly how *you* felt when you received this grade. How were *you* feeling before you began to think about your parents' reaction?"

As a counselor, it made no difference to Ben if the students were proud of themselves or disappointed in themselves. The only thing that mattered was that students answered honestly. As long as an answer is truthful, it reflects honest self-evaluation by the students. If students were pleased with themselves, Ben would follow up with questions like: "Do you like feeling like this? Do you know what you need to do to maintain this positive feeling? Do you know what you did to be so successful? Is it worth doing again? Would you like to feel this good again? All the time? Are you willing to work hard enough to maintain the good feelings that you have?" All of these questions, and all of the variations that you can think of, help kids develop responsibility and become better decision makers.

The same approach works just as well when students are disappointed in themselves. Ben would ask: "You don't feel so good about this, huh? Would you like to feel better? Do you have any idea about what you need to do differently to feel better? Can you do it? Do you need some help? If so, do you know where to get it, and are you going to get the help you need? Do you believe that you have some control over how you feel?" That last question is especially important. Some students see no connection between what they do and how they feel. That is the epitome of powerlessness: to believe that our actions are unrelated to our happiness and satisfaction. When we meet such students, our first priority is to help them see a connection between what they do and how they feel. Until students develop a sense of control in their lives, they will be at great risk in virtually every area of their existence, academically and socially.

Despite his enthusiasm, Ben found that some of his counselees found his new approach somewhat unsettling. "How come you don't tell our parents they should get us something special when we do our work?" "It's not so easy talking with you anymore. You make us think!" There were times when Ben was tempted to revert to rewarding and threatening and allowing everyone to see him as the architect of successful intervention strategies. What kept him from going back was staying focused on his new picture of what he wanted for himself as a counselor.

Though Ben struggled, he was committed to doing what he thought was best for kids in the long run and best for himself in his attempt to be a quality counselor. As Ben began to counsel using the principles of internal control, he came to understand the importance of building a strong, trusting relationship with kids. His previous style was not especially relationship-dependent. He focused on the problem and the solution, not the student. As Ben began to ask evaluation questions, a strong relationship became essential. You don't have to be particularly connected to another to tell them what to do. But genuine conversation involving honest self-evaluation demands a strong relationship. Once Ben started tapping into internal motivation, he appreciated the importance of relationships.

Especially at first, taking the time to build a strong connection with kids was hard for Ben. As he talked with a student in his office, his mind wandered and conjured up unpleasant visions of a growing line of kids waiting to see him. On more than one occasion Ben rushed kids without giving them the time they needed. It always caught up with him when those "rushed" kids ended up costing more time down the road with ongoing, usually increased, difficulty. Soon Ben realized that spending a few extra minutes with kids, especially as he was just getting to know them, saved considerable time later on. Perhaps more importantly, the connections they were building enabled Ben to ask the tough self-evaluation questions that have become his trademark.

As a counselor, the kids aren't Ben's only "clients." He helps teachers do their jobs better, too. When Ben switched to counseling using internal control psychology, not every teacher was ecstatic. For years, Ben had been a favorite of the teachers. They'd have a problem, Ben would structure an intervention strategy, and the kids would perform better. But as Ben had discovered, the improvement was only temporary. Using a counseling approach based on internal control psychology, Ben found that some kids chose to do better. Others continued to underachieve. He took each situation and did everything possible to make it a learning experience for the kids. It didn't always result in immediate academic improvement. What sustained Ben was staying focused on his internal picture and being clear about his role. Part of Ben's job is to help students become responsible decision makers. By helping kids process the consequences of their actions and allowing them to take an appropriate level of responsibility, he was doing his job well.

Fortunately for Ben, he had been in the district for a long time and had strong working relationships with most of his colleagues. As he changed his counseling style, they were able to talk about their respective roles and responsibilities with kids. Once teachers knew that Ben was motivated by a desire to help kids become responsible decision makers, most of them were able to more comfortably tolerate some continued noncompliance and underachievement by their students.

Throughout the rest of that school year, Ben continued to counsel using the concepts of internal motivation. Ben abandoned his behavior modification programs, instead asking kids to evaluate their behavior at almost every opportunity. While he had less short-term success, Ben was convinced that kids who turned things around had made "real" change. Students who started to do better seemed genuinely pleased to have chosen a different set of behaviors. They seemed to enjoy school more. Before, Ben had kids who were more compliant but who still disliked school. Now, Ben sensed that kids who had made positive changes really felt better about themselves. The teachers confirmed his suspicions. Even some of the more skeptical teachers said they saw more genuine improvement in academic performance and attitude than in previous years. This feedback kept Ben going for the rest of the school year.

The real key was to see how Ben's counselees did once they got to the high school. The following school year, soon after the first marking period, there was a meeting between the middle school counselors and the high school counselors. Everyone was interested in finding out how well the middle school kids were doing in the high school, both academically and socially.

Ben was nervous when the meeting began. He had made a huge switch in the past year. He had changed his whole approach with kids and abandoned a style that had won him favor with colleagues and a positive reputation built over 15 years. Ben was about to learn whether his efforts made a difference. He was incredibly pleased to hear the high school counselors say without reservation that his former counselees were the most prepared group they had encountered. They were significantly more responsible and successful than the kids he had sent up in prior years. All the work Ben had done was worth the effort! As the discussion took place, he found himself drifting back to the year before, when they had a similar meeting. At that time, Ben had felt incompetent as he learned how poorly his counselees were doing once they arrived in high school. This year, he felt both competent and satisfied.

Commentary

Power is the most misunderstood basic need. When Ben began to learn internal control psychology, he ascribed a negative value to the term "power." As someone who had dedicated his professional life to helping others, he didn't see himself as driven by power. When Ben expanded his definition of power to include competence, he quickly realized that he was, indeed, a counselor with a strong need for power. Ben worked hard to develop a positive reputation, and he wanted to be perceived as competent.

The reward-punishment approach that Ben had used for so long provided short-term success but nothing more. As long as Ben was there to hold the carrot or stick in front of his counselees, they were compliant. Once they moved to the high school, beyond Ben's immediate sphere of influence, they reverted to their irresponsible, unsuccessful ways.

Ben vigorously engaged in a process of self-evaluation that helped him grow as a counselor. The most important shift Ben made was redrawing the lines of responsibility. Previously, Ben evaluated his success or failure on what *others* did. Once he learned internal control psychology, Ben began to evaluate himself on his own behavior, not the behavior of others. He began to take responsibility for what *he* did while letting students take responsibility for what *they* did.

This shift is especially important for anyone who works with a high-risk population. If you evaluate your success on the behaviors of others and they fail, you are keeping yourself in a position of powerlessness. As competent as you may be, you *cannot* control the actions of another. To evaluate yourself on their choices is a recipe for burnout.

Develop a clear picture of your role and the accompanying responsibilities. Given the expectations of your role and your expectations of yourself as a professional, have you been successful? This does not mean that you don't care about the success of those you work with. Rather, it means that you have defined the lines of responsibility and evaluated yourself on what you can do, not on what others choose to do.

Ben discovered that his counselees didn't always like to self-evaluate. Many of them preferred it when he told them what to do. Self-evaluation and taking responsibility is hard work. Many of us would rather have someone else tell us what to do. It's easier and does not require us to take responsibility for our lives. Despite the reluctance of his counselees, Ben was able to maintain his resolve because he kept his role and goal in mind. He knew he wanted to help students develop a sense of responsibility, and he wanted to inspire lasting change.

Finally, Ben reminds us that he serves teachers as well as students. Ben's new approach meant that some students didn't change as much in the short run, even if the changes were more effective over time. Because teachers didn't reap the benefits of short-term success, Ben needed to make sure they understood what he was doing. Over his career, Ben had built positive relationships with his middle school colleagues, and he was able to tell them he was helping students develop a sense of responsibility and the ability to be good decision makers. By creating a shared picture with his colleagues, Ben enlisted their support, even though it meant some students were less successful in the short term. Had Ben not communicated with his colleagues, they would have perceived him as less effective.

What You Can Do

- Get a clear picture of your role and goal.
- Decide if you are looking for short-term success or lasting change. The reward-punishment model almost always provides more immediate success.
- If you are working toward lasting change, ask self-evaluation questions instead of prescribing a course of action.
- Take responsibility for your behavior and let others take responsibility for theirs.
- Evaluate yourself based upon your role and responsibilities, not on the choices of others and situations over which you have no control. If you don't, you will remain powerless.
- When you ask others to self-evaluate, expect them to be resistant. People often prefer to be told what to do because they don't have to take responsibility.
- If you are a counselor, remember that you serve teachers as well as students. To be successful, develop a shared vision of success with your colleagues as well as with your counselees.

Chapter 9

Inspiring Through Collaboration

When I met Ron at a conference a couple of years ago, I was immediately impressed by his energy, enthusiasm, and effectiveness. If I were asked to describe this middle school principal in a word, it would be "magnetic." Ron was more than a "charmer." He was genuine. He had brought several of his teachers with him, and the workshop they led describing the success of their 600-student middle school was professional, supported by action research, and involving. Ron was someone I knew could add to this story by telling *his* story.

Before speaking with Ron, I approached a couple of the teachers who had been his copresenters. I asked Sandy and Glenn what it was like to work for Ron. Right away, I learned that Ron was different from most administrators. "You don't work *for* Ron," Sandy answered quickly. "You work *with* him. He made a big deal out of that when he hired me. I can be cynical, and I wasn't convinced by his words. But once I started working at the school, it was clear that Ron really did strive to be more collaborative than any other administrator I have known."

"I was already at the school when Ron arrived," Glenn added. "I remember him saying the same thing to the whole staff the first time he addressed us. It was clear from the beginning that Ron was going to be different."

I asked Glenn to amplify.

"We were a pretty traditional school. None of us knew Ron. He was coming from another district. Our only knowledge about him was what we saw on paper and what we learned during the hiring process. We had no reason to expect he was going to be especially different from what we had always known. Anyway, it was clear from our first staff meeting that Ron was going to be a really different kind of experience."

"What did he do that was so different?" I asked.

"The thing we noticed right away was the room arrangement for our first staff meeting. We were used to sitting classroom style, in rows, with the principal at the front of the room. When we walked into our first meeting with Ron, he had the room arranged in a large circle with exactly the right number of chairs. Of course, the first thing we had to figure out was where the front of the circle was! I think we were all worried we were going to sit in the principal's chair and get things started off on the wrong foot. I remember us hesitating until someone asked Ron which seat was his. 'I'll sit in whatever chair is empty,' he answered. When we began, Ron addressed the room configuration and gave his very brief '*with* not *for*' address. He told us that he had chosen to have us sit in a circle 'because there is no front of the room in a circle.' He wanted our first meeting together to physically emphasize that we were a team, working collaboratively toward a common goal. He said there would be times he would have something to tell us that would better lend itself to a different configuration, but he told us he still preferred a large horseshoe so we could see each other and interact more effectively."

"What else did he say that was different?" I asked.

Glenn continued, "What made Ron stand out from the first day was what he *didn't say* and *didn't do*. He didn't share his vision with us. He didn't encourage us to arrange our classrooms in a circle. He didn't preach to us. He just told us he wanted to collaborate and that he wanted a great school where we loved coming to work." Glenn paused a moment. "During that first meeting, Ron never mentioned the kids or the parents. He's probably the most student-centered educator I've ever met, but that day he never talked about the kids. He didn't say much. It was a quick meeting, something we all appreciated since school was starting in a day and we were primarily interested in going to our rooms and getting organized. The little he said was about us. About working together and enjoying our jobs. He didn't mention test scores. He didn't mention getting involved in extracurricular activities. He didn't mention finding ways to involve the parents and community. He didn't mention homework, or grading, or discipline. Just us. Then he told us he imagined we all had to get ready for the first day of school so he was done. He said he would be around to chat or answer questions, but he didn't want to cut into the precious little time we had. At the time, we thought it was a little strange. A new principal, his first time addressing the staff, and so little to say. In retrospect, we discovered that Ron did two incredibly important things during that meeting. First, he modeled everything. As a leader, Ron believes he should *show* rather than *tell*. He did that with the seating arrangement and by respecting our professionalism and giving us maximum time to do our jobs well. The other thing he did was focus on *us* and let us know that building a professional learning community where people loved their jobs was his priority."

"OK," I said. "But I'm curious about how you got to where you are now. I attended your presentation today. You talked about action research. You talked about test scores. You talked about parent and community involvement. You talked about the absence of disruption in your school. You talked about all those things that Ron *didn't* talk about when he met you! How did you get there?"

"Wait a minute," said Sandy. "I want to add one piece before you get into that topic. It's a vignette about my interview with Ron when I was hired. It was like that first staff meeting Glenn mentioned, except it was just Ron and I in his office. Right away I was struck by a couple of things. Like most principals, Ron has a desk and a few chairs for visitors who come to his office. I expected he would sit behind his desk during the interview. Instead, he sat in one of the 'regular' chairs with me, with no desk separating us to affirm his authority. Ron immediately created the sense that I would be working *with*, not *for* him. The other thing is that Ron asked me what I liked to do for fun, what my interests were. He asked about my attitude toward kids. Middle school kids are going through potentially difficult developmental things, and Ron was interested in what I knew about early adolescent development and my attitude toward working with kids who might be problematic. Ron is passionate about middle school and thinks that middle school kids and middle school teachers are sometimes perceived negatively. He asked me, 'If I offered you a job right now teaching social studies in the middle school or the high school, which one would you choose?' I believe I was hired because I answered 'middle school' with no hesitation."

"What did Ron ask you about instruction and pedagogy?" I asked. "Did he refer to your transcript or experience?"

"Nothing directly," Sandy replied. "By asking about me and my attitude toward kids, especially early adolescents, Ron was assessing if I was a person who would fit well with the staff and school. He was finding out if I was philosophically aligned with where the school was headed. And he found out that I was a person who genuinely liked kids and wanted to love my job."

"So content and pedagogy doesn't mean much to Ron?" I asked.

"That's where you're wrong," Sandy answered. "Ron just didn't emphasize those issues, especially initially. He believes that it's more important to hire the right people, people with positive attitudes toward kids and work, than look for candidates with the most impressive transcripts and resumes. Ron believes he can help us develop our *teaching* skills with relative ease if we bring a positive attitude to school with us. But that's not to say Ron doesn't value sound instructional practice. We're constantly looking at data to improve our instructional effectiveness. Don't get fooled by Ron's easy demeanor. He cares very much about student achievement and works hard to maintain parent and community support. There is one last thing about the interview."

"What's that?"

"You asked about transcripts and resumes. Even though Ron never mentioned any of that during our interview, at least a half-dozen times during my first year he made comments that made it obvious he had thoroughly read my application packet and he was very familiar with things I had studied and what I was bringing to the school. Ron didn't ask me about those things during the interview because he already had that information documented. He had already studied it, and he didn't want to waste time asking me about what he already knew! Instead, he concentrated on *me as a person and my attitude toward kids,* things that could not possibly be captured by any of the documents he had in front of him. Ron appears casual and relaxed, but he is purposeful in how he acts."

"Sandy, by the time you were hired, the school had already become one where fostering internal motivation was established and implemented by the teachers and staff. I imagine that was discussed during the interview," I said.

"Wrong again!" replied Sandy with a good-natured laugh. "Ron never mentioned it. And thank goodness he didn't. I knew very little about internal control psychology. It was mentioned tangentially in a 'methods of teaching' class, but I couldn't discuss it in depth. Plus, if I had been questioned about it, I would have felt uncomfortable. It would have seemed very cultlike if Ron started talking about internal control psychology and had announced, 'This is what we do here.'"

"Then how did he know you would mesh with the culture he was in the process of creating?" I asked. "Wasn't he afraid you would represent a 'bad hire' if you didn't subscribe to the underlying psychology that drives the school?"

Sandy said, "You'll have to ask Ron how worried he was. As for me, if we had had a discussion about internal control psychology, all Ron would have learned was that I didn't know much about it. I'm not sure that would have helped him. If he had then started to explain it to me, it would have been an incredible turnoff during an interview. I wasn't there to hear a lecture, even about something I have come to value. I was there to interview for a teaching position!"

"That makes sense," I agreed. "But I'm still not sure how Ron was certain you'd be a good match for the school."

Sandy continued, "When Ron asked about me, my interests, and my attitude toward kids and teaching, he learned enough about me to know I would fit in with the school philosophy and the internal motivation orientation that Ron values."

Glenn had been listening intently. "There's something else that will help you understand Ron better," he said. "He has never asked people to align themselves with internal control psychology. In fact, I don't know if Ron has ever even encouraged it. He'll talk about it at length to anyone who is interested. He'll lend us and buy us books. But one reason why virtually everyone believes in the ideas of internal motivation in our school is precisely because it has never been mandated!" Glenn started laughing. "Imagine that. Telling the staff that they are internally motivated and then mandating that they all conform to one way of looking at the world!"

"Exactly!" exclaimed Sandy. "Ron has his 'nonnegotiables,' but they are not related to a specific psychology or theory. They are related to liking kids, understanding developmental issues, having energy and enthusiasm for teaching, and wanting to grow professionally and love your job. If you have those qualities, you'll be fine here. And if you have those qualities, you'll probably discover that learning and applying internal control psychology will be helpful. It's not a mandate; it's something we want to do. And Ron facilitates that for us."

The more I listened to Sandy and Glenn, the more impressed I was by Ron. He was clearly more than a charismatic personality. He was an intelligent, organized leader who had built a high-performing school where teachers loved their jobs. I remained unclear about how Ron helped move the school in that direction. "OK," I said. "I went to your workshop. I'm convinced you have a great school and people love their jobs and kids are achieving. I'm convinced that things are different from how they used to be. I'm convinced that Ron is a skilled principal who has nurtured this. How did he do it?"

"That," Sandy said, "is something you'll have to ask Ron."

"The good news," Glenn added, "is that Ron will be happy to talk with you, I'm sure. That's one of the reasons we're here.

He wanted the chance to connect with more people. Just tell him you'd like to talk, and he'll share his story. I bet you'll find it interesting and a little surprising."

Glenn was right—on both counts. Ron was more than willing to talk, and his story was something different from what I expected.

• • •

"Ron, it's a pleasure to meet you," I said. "I've spoken with Sandy and Glenn. They certainly have a lot of respect for you. I really appreciate you talking with me."

"My pleasure," said Ron. "I have just one stipulation."

"What's that?" I asked.

"I'll tell you some of the things we've done that have helped us taste some success as long as you promise me you'll include what I did poorly in my last position."

"Sure, but you must admit that's a pretty unusual request," I countered.

"No doubt," said Ron. "But I think that giving people a sense of the things I did incorrectly might be more helpful than simply throwing a few accolades our way. It's no secret that you can't achieve success by simply mimicking what's been done, so our success with kids might not be particularly instructive anyway. On the other hand, I think you can get a lot out of hearing about the failures of another so you don't make the same mistakes."

I had been with Ron for just a few minutes, and already I was aware of something that set him apart. Whenever Ron spoke of success, he used the terms "we," "our," and "us"; when he spoke of shortcomings, he referred only to himself. He was very quick to share the glory and equally willing to take full responsibility for the mistakes. What made all of this remarkable was that it struck me as completely genuine. I didn't get the sense that it was an affectation.

"OK," I said. "Let's start with how you moved your school forward. You came to the school as an unknown, and within a few years student achievement has improved dramatically. Teachers are enthusiastic. The community supports the school. You must have done something right!"

"Sure, I was instrumental in our success. I'm not saying I haven't played an important role. As building principal, I am a key figure in our success. But I am clear on what my role is and how I can best contribute to our school becoming more successful. Let me draw a distinction between a visionary and a leader. A visionary is someone who has a well-defined picture of quality and who functions primarily as a delegator, assigning tasks so the vision is brought to fruition. I see myself as a leader. As a leader, I have a less defined picture of quality. In fact, I want to keep my picture intentionally vague. Whereas a visionary is specific and can tell you in precise terms what a quality school might look like, an effective leader is only able to give you general descriptors of quality. For example, I know I want a school where teachers love kids, love their jobs, are willing to stretch and grow, work collaboratively, and see the parents and community as allies in the quest to bring the best possible educational experience to the kids. Great stuff—and pretty vague. There's nothing aligned with a particular school of thought or philosophy or approach. It's intentionally vague so it can be fully inclusive."

"What would you see as the primary role of the leader, if not to provide a detailed picture of quality?"

"I provide the broad strokes, the general descriptors that facilitate flexibility and creativity. The leader's job is to create the environment so the staff fully participates and collectively builds a highly defined, collaborative picture of quality. I won't minimize what we've done. It's the cooperative learning adage put into action: 'All of us is smarter than any one of us.' No matter how insightful and committed I might be, the school *we* are creating and the vision that *we* continue to grow is more complete and has more substance than anything I might have envisioned on my own. That's why I'm a proponent of collaboration. It's not because working together *feels good*. If it felt good and the results were mediocre, then collaboration wouldn't be worth the effort. Collaboration is valuable because it helps us transcend our individual limits and create something greater than ourselves. It takes incredible energy and commitment, but getting a staff to collaborate is the most inspiring thing I've ever experienced."

"How did you do it?" I asked. "I understand that you can't give me a formula that others can simply copy, but there must be a few things that you can share that others can use as starting points."

"Sure. I can give you a number of ideas, provided people understand that these are strategies that worked for *us*. They may need to be modified to be effective for someone else. Also, my ideas may work for us because I believe in them. Another leader may have different ideas and strategies that work equally well. All I can share is *a way*, not *the way*.

"My strongest recommendation to anyone in a leadership position is to start small and be focused. It's not unusual for a new leader to have a host of ideas and initiatives that they would like to see implemented. There is a temptation to try to impress the staff by introducing lots of innovative practices. My advice is to pare your list down to the minimum. After you've done that, cut it some more! You may think that you are sacrificing a chance to show your staff how bright you are, but I think you will be better off doing as little as possible.

"Glenn told you about our first staff meeting. That's an example of keeping things small and focused. I wanted the group to sit in a circle, to actually *see* one another as we met, and to introduce the concept of collaboration. The other thing I especially liked about that introductory meeting was avoiding all the things the staff expected to hear. I didn't talk about the kids. I'm a passionate advocate for kids and high academic achievement, but at that point I was more interested in the staff knowing that I was *their* advocate.

"The first month I was principal, I never uttered anything that could be interpreted as criticism. As someone who believes in internal motivation, I'm not big on praise either, because it's usually used to control others. Still, whenever I saw anything that I liked, be it in the classroom, cafeteria, hallways, or anywhere else, I acknowledged it. People appreciate being acknowledged when they know it's genuine and not done to manipulate."

"What's the difference between *praising* and *acknowledging*?" I asked.

"Praise is often used to control people and get them to do what you want. Acknowledgment implies less external control. Just as importantly, whenever I acknowledged something, I would ask the person what *they* thought and how *they* felt about the situation. I was consciously trying to move the focus from an external orientation to one based on internal motivation. If people discovered that *they* felt good doing something, that would be more meaningful than simply getting verbal reinforcement from the boss."

"Didn't you see anything that troubled you in that first month?" I asked.

"Of course I did!" exclaimed Ron. "Along with all the wonderful things I saw and heard, I was hearing and seeing things that weren't aligned with my central values. As the principal, I needed to decide if focusing on the negative was going to help us become a better school. I believed that would have been counterproductive. It would have created an adversarial relationship with staff. I would have forfeited any hope of gaining their trust. I might have succeeded in getting them to comply, but I never would have won their hearts and got them to bring out their creativity. They would have been so worried about how to avoid getting in trouble with 'the boss' that they never would have become superior teachers. So I consciously decided to nurture a positive, trusting relationship. It wasn't easy. I've had lots of practice being impatient! It's easy for me to slip into a coercive mode and even convince myself that I'm doing it 'for your own good'! But I was committed to cultivating a positive environment, so I waited for teachable moments."

"Give me an example of one of these 'teachable moments,' Ron."

"After we had a few staff meetings, one of the teachers came to see me with a concern. She was wondering what I was going to do about Helen, a teacher in the school. I admitted I was confused, as I was unaware of what Helen was doing that was so horrible that a colleague would come to the principal. She told me that she found it 'completely disrespectful' that Helen knitted throughout our staff meetings. She said she was coming to me because I was a new principal and she wanted me to be successful, and she thought it was important that I let the staff know right away that disrespect was not tolerated.

"As you might have guessed, the 'informant' was a veteran teacher who adhered to a traditional approach to teaching and learning. I told her I appreciated her support and that I would be sure to speak with Helen.

"A few days later, I spoke with Helen and commented that I had noticed her knitting during the recent staff meeting. Specifically, I asked her what she was making and asked if she had been knitting a long time or if it was a hobby she had recently taken up. During our conversation, Helen thanked me for not reprimanding her for knitting. 'Why would I do that?' I asked. 'Our last principal had a strict rule against anything like that,' she replied. 'He said we were on company time and we should be giving him our undivided attention.' I asked Helen what she thought of that. 'That's the funny thing!' she exclaimed. 'I agree with him! When I knit, I am better able to pay attention. With nothing to do with my hands, I drift off. Of course, I did what he wanted and stopped knitting, but I swear I was less attentive.'

"I then told Helen that her former principal was not alone, that there were staff members who might think her knitting was 'disrespectful.' I asked Helen if she would be willing to informally address the staff at our next meeting and let them know that knitting helped her stay more appropriately focused. I assured Helen that she didn't have to address the staff if she were uncomfortable, but I thought it would be helpful for them to have accurate information. Helen clearly appreciated the chance to address her colleagues. 'I would never want them to think I was acting unprofessionally. I just hope I don't sound defensive when I tell them that knitting helps me focus on what is being said.'"

"How is that a 'teachable moment'?" I asked Ron.

"When Helen addressed the staff at our next meeting, it

inspired a discussion about how kids learn differently from each other and how we sometimes misinterpret their behaviors. What we discussed has led to finding ways to help more kids pay attention effectively in classes. We've discovered that not as many kids have 'attention problems' as we thought. We've found ways to reach more kids, and suddenly their attention has improved! If I had given the staff a formal presentation about learning styles and encouraged them to find ways to engage kids who were struggling, it would have been less effective. By taking advantage of the 'teachable moment' that presented itself, the staff discussed something important with more energy and commitment and no coercion from me."

"Given your affinity for internal control psychology, when and how did you introduce that to your staff?" I asked.

"I never tried to introduce any of that to the staff. I just worked on building our professional relationships and doing what I could to get them to trust themselves and me. Over time, staff members asked if I had any books I would recommend. At those times, I would lend them books that emphasized internal control and motivation. I was careful not to push anything. Some of the staff asked if we could dedicate some professional development time to learning about internal motivation and how to apply it within the school. Those sessions were well received, and some staff decided to involve themselves in more in-depth workshops. I was supportive, but I was clear that no one was 'required' to study internal control psychology."

"Weren't you worried that the teachers might not want to learn something you valued?" I asked. "Wasn't there a risk in being noncoercive?"

"I don't think so," Ron answered. "Maybe you're right. But it was essential to me that I be noncoercive about studying internal motivation. The 'nonnegotiables' I have involve caring about kids, valuing student achievement, and working collaboratively in a joyful environment. My credibility would be destroyed if I suggested that there was only one way to proceed and I knew the way. I had to build a strong relationship with my staff and trust that they would gravitate toward internal control psychology if it made sense to them. As you know, they have taken to it and we are continuing to build an even better school for kids and staff. I don't particularly care what label we use. I only care that we're building a school where kids learn as much as they can, and teachers love coming to work and appreciate the opportunity to inspire kids every day by tapping into the internal motivation that kids bring with them to school each and every day."

I thanked Ron for his time and for all the information he had shared. "Wait," he said. "We're not done yet. You promised me I could tell you about my last position and how poorly I did."

"Oh, yes," I said. "I had forgotten. Remind me again why it will be helpful to rehash your mistakes."

"Because I did some typical things with some predictably disastrous results. If telling others what I did wrong helps a few people avoid those errors, that would be a good thing."

"OK, Ron. Let's hear it."

"In a nutshell, when I learned about internal control psychology, without realizing it, I became a zealot. I thought I was being enthusiastic. But I was overbearing. I thought I was sharing something really wonderful with my staff. In reality, I was giving them information they didn't want. I was a visionary, but I was the only one with the vision. Because others didn't see what I saw, I assumed I was right and they were uninformed. The more I tried to inform them, to 'save' them, the more they resisted me."

"What turned it around?" I asked.

"Nothing," answered Ron. "For a year or two, I kept trying to make it happen. The more I tried, the worse it got. Morale was horrible. Whereas I saw myself as an enthusiastic leader, the teachers saw me as an arrogant pain in the ass. Because I went about everything the wrong way, I could never inspire them. By the time I realized how foolish I had been, I knew it was too late for me to be a real leader in that school. Fortunately, this job opened up, I applied, and I was lucky enough to be selected as the principal. I made myself a promise that the second time around I would act like a leader instead of a zealot. When I reflect upon the progress we have made together, I know it was the right decision."

I thoroughly enjoyed my time with Ron. It would have been easy for him to simply recount how he had led his current staff on their journey toward increased quality. He was, however, someone who wanted to help others experience quality without having to undergo some of the difficulty he had experienced. Ron was able to harness his enthusiasm and passion and become a successful noncoercive leader who continues to inspire his staff. The result is a school where staff are happy and kids are thriving academically and socially.

Commentary

Ron's passion for education and his boundless energy were not enough for him to be the successful leader he has become. Ron's success was due to several key factors. First, Ron made sure that his staff perceived him as an advocate. Too many schools are characterized by divisiveness between administration and the teaching staff. During his initial meeting with his teachers, Ron began to build a partnership.

Every principal needs the support of the staff to succeed. It doesn't matter how intelligent, energetic, or committed the principal is, there will be no success without the support of teachers. Knowing that, Ron built alliances. Teachers who are genuinely valued and supported will work hard to make a school successful.

Ron modeled what he valued. During his initial meeting with teachers, he arranged the room in a circle because that configuration supported the collaboration he wanted to foster. Rather than just saying it, Ron put his beliefs into practice. Even though Ron believed in the principles of internal control psychology, he never pushed these ideas. Instead, Ron "lived" the principles, and teachers came to value internal control psychology in a natural, comfortable way.

Ron treated his teachers with respect. His meetings were as long as necessary but not a minute longer, because he respected that teachers had other important things to do. Leaders who respect their teachers will get their respect and support in return.

In every interaction with his staff, Ron nurtured the positive relationships needed for success. Even when he saw things he didn't like, Ron was wise enough to know when to address issues and when to let things slide. He kept his goals in mind and took action that helped him move in the direction he was trying to go. His steadfast commitment to a goal helped Ron lead with a sense of purpose rather than stumble as impediments continually presented themselves.

Ron's success was based, in part, on his definition of leadership. He articulated a broad goal, one large and inviting enough that all teachers could make a meaningful contribution. By fostering true collaboration and engaging the staff, Ron inspired energy that transformed the school.

What You Can Do

• Build a positive relationship with your staff. The staff needs to know that you care before they care what you know.

• Make certain that your staff sees you as an advocate. When they see you as an ally, they will work hard for you. If they don't see you as an ally, they will be driven by the need to survive, not the need to become more competent.

• Model what you value. Your actions should mirror your words.

• Take advantage of all the "teachable moments" that present themselves. This makes your leadership relevant and less abstract.

• Invite genuine collaboration. Teachers give their best effort when it makes a difference.

• Celebrate the success that comes from many hands working in harmony.

Chapter 10

Being What We Choose

A bright and successful student in 8th grade, Tiffany had struggled in the 6th and 7th grades and was dangerously close to being retained or going to summer school. Her mother's attempts to be helpful had actually enabled Tiffany to maintain her irresponsible orientation until she was helped by her school counselor. I asked Tiffany to tell me what had helped her develop into the successful student she had become.

"Learning about internal motivation helped me a lot," Tiffany began. "Especially how my guidance counselor used it with me. I went through some rough times at school for a couple of years. Now I'm finishing up 8th grade and getting ready to go to high school. I feel good about myself, and I'm confident that I'll be a successful student in high school and beyond."

"Tiffany," I asked, "how was your counselor helpful?"

"When adults talked to me, they always asked what I was *doing*. As a matter of fact, when an adult asked what I was doing, it usually meant I was in trouble because I wasn't doing what they wanted! My guidance counselor was really different. As soon as we met, she made me feel like I was really important and that what I wanted to *be* was really interesting. She asked questions about the kind of person I admired and the kind of person I wanted to be. I used words like 'smart' and 'successful' and 'trustworthy' and 'real' and 'not a slacker.' She asked what those words meant *to me*. I'm used to adults telling me the definitions of words, but my guidance counselor asks me what *I mean*. I feel important when I talk with her."

"Would you say your counselor was always on your side?" I asked.

"I'm not sure about that," Tiffany said. "It wasn't like she was trying to be my friend. Even though she makes me feel important, she's not easy on me. When I was doing bad in school, especially at the beginning of 7th grade, she kept asking me if I was *being trustworthy, being successful, being smart, not being a slacker*. She never asked me what I was *doing*. She never asked me about my *feelings* or if I liked my teachers. She just kept asking me who I was *being* and if that's who I wanted to be. Because I respect her and trust her, I told her the truth. I guess she was on my side because she wanted what was best for me. But she didn't accept everything I did. She had me look at everything I did and decide if I was being who I wanted to be. I liked that she never told me what to do. She just kept asking who I wanted to *be*."

"You make it sound like this helped you a lot," I said.

"It did. As soon as I focused on who I wanted to be, I started doing really good in school. My grades went way up, even with teachers I didn't like. That's another thing I really like about my counselor. She never tried to get me to like my teachers. She understood that I liked some teachers and I didn't like others. She just asked me if I wanted to be 'successful' or 'successful only with teachers you like.' The one time my guidance counselor ever *told* me anything directly was when I started to complain about some of my teachers. She said if I acted the way I wanted to be only with people I liked, I was letting other people control me. She said I was letting people I didn't like keep me from being smart and successful. I'll never forget what she told me. She said, 'Tiffany, you have to decide if you want to be a successful person or if you are going to give up being successful when you meet people you don't like.'"

"Did her comment help you?"

"It makes sense now, but when she first said it to me I didn't want to hear it. I wanted to make excuses and blame other people when I wasn't doing good. My guidance counselor, even though she's wicked nice, wouldn't let me do that. She got me past making excuses. Every day I tell myself that I want to be smart, successful, trustworthy, and not a slacker. I want to be that whether I have good teachers or teachers I don't like. I've decided that I'm going to be who I want to be even if I don't always have the teachers I want. I know I'm motivated from the inside and I can choose how I want to be."

"I know you are having a good year, Tiffany," I said. "What have your teachers done to help make it a successful year for you?"

"Most of my teachers are pretty awesome. They tell us what we have to know and do to be successful in their class, but they give us choices about how to do it. I like having choices, and I know my friends do, too."

"Are you saying teachers should let kids do what they want?" I asked.

"No," Tiffany answered. "It might sound kind of weird, but I think sometimes teachers should tell us what we have to do and not give us a choice. Kids love it when they have a choice, but we need teachers to be in charge and keep us focused. If teachers let kids do whatever they want, most kids would just goof around and not learn very much. I think good teachers give some choices but keep kids focused. We want teachers who listen to us and respect us. But we need teachers to make sure we don't get out of control."

"What else makes a good teacher?" I asked Tiffany.

"One cool thing that one of my teachers did this year was, instead of telling us the rules like most teachers do, he had us create a class constitution. The class came up with rules and ideas about how we should behave to make the class good. Every kid was part of the discussion, and we all signed the constitution. Even though kids can get rowdy, no one ever goofs around in that class. I think it's because we all made up our own constitution, so we just follow it. It's real different than having someone else tell you what to do, even if you end up with the same rules."

"Do you have any complaints about your teachers, Tiffany?"

"Some teachers still do things that drive me crazy. I used to let that keep me from doing good in school, but now it's not a big deal. I want to be a successful student even with a not-so-good teacher. I figure when I get to high school and college, I'll have some teachers I might not like so much. At least now I know that no matter what, I can choose to be successful. I'm glad my guidance counselor helped me figure that out last year. I think that's the most important lesson I'll ever learn in school."

Commentary

Nathan, the 4th grade student from Chapter 6, was primarily driven by the cooperative needs. He talked about how much he liked his classroom because it was fun. As an adolescent, Tiffany is more driven by the needs for power and freedom. Her counselor wisely asks Tiffany to identify the kind of person she wants to be, honoring her autonomy and the power inherent in choosing an identity. Identity formation is the primary developmental task of adolescence. When the counselor asks Tiffany to determine who she wants to be and to evaluate her behavior with that picture in mind, she nurtures Tiffany's development. Adolescence is an ideal time to ask evaluation questions that focus on "being." By focusing on "being," Tiffany's counselor indirectly helps her evaluate what behaviors are congruent with her internal picture of who she wants to be (trustworthy, successful, smart, not a slacker).

Even though adolescents are strongly driven by the needs for power and freedom, Tiffany's story illustrates the ongoing importance of relationship and belonging. She trusts her counselor, and it is their strong relationship that allows Tiffany to successfully navigate a difficult time.

Tiffany liked creating a class constitution. This activity allows students to determine classroom rules and how they want to treat each other to support learning. While it is always helpful to have students involved in the formation of classroom rules, it is especially important in middle school. Developmentally, middle school students are appreciative of opportunities to have power and freedom. The self-governing quality of creating a classroom constitution is need-satisfying and leads to learning environments that are characterized by less disruption and more academic achievement.

Tiffany was lucky. She did poorly in both 6th grade and 7th grade. Many young students who struggle at an early age are identified as academic failures and never discover that they can be successful. Others are pushed and prodded and rewarded for minimal compliance, stuck in a cycle of failure. Tiffany was fortunate to have teachers, a counselor, and parents who helped her learn from her mistake and build an identity as a successful student. Every student deserves the chance that Tiffany got.

What You Can Do

• Give adolescents as much power as possible. They crave it and will seek it in potentially inappropriate and dangerous ways if they don't have enough. Equipping your students with academic competence will help them achieve power in a responsible way.

• Give students choices without compromising high standards.

• Provide structure and control within an environment that allows for some choices. Students need to have adequate self-control to manage freedom appropriately. If you give students more freedom than they can responsibly manage, your classroom will be characterized by chaos.

• Remember that adolescents need to feel a sense of belonging with important adults. Maintain positive relationships even when adolescents are behaving in less-than-graceful ways.

• Give adolescents opportunities to discover who they want to be. Given their developmental imperative, it is better to focus on who they want to *be* than on what they want to *do*.

Part IV

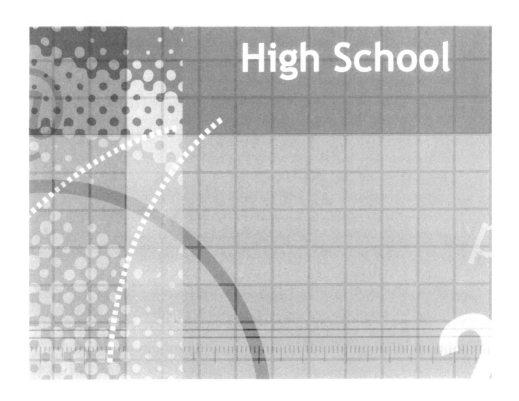

High School

Chapter 11

Creating a Need-Satisfying Environment

Dave had taught high school English for about 10 years when he first learned about internal control psychology. In courses he had taken both as an undergraduate and as a graduate student, the emphasis was on external motivation and how to "make" kids succeed by using the right blend of rewards and punishment. When Dave got his first teaching position, his supervisors appeared more interested in his ability to control the class than in his ability to teach students. As long as there weren't behavior problems in his classes, Dave was considered a good teacher.

Having always been interested in psychology and motivation, Dave enrolled in a workshop about internal motivation and immediately saw that he could use the concepts to teach literature. It was a natural, easy fit. Because of his keen interest in motivation, Dave especially enjoyed learning about the basic needs that drive our behavior.

Dave quickly integrated internal control psychology into his teaching of literature and found that students developed more insightful comments once equipped with an understanding of how fictional characters, like real people, are motivated from the inside out. Dave and his students engaged in substantive conversation about the needs that motivated the characters they encountered and the conflicting wants that created dramatic tension in a story. Hawthorne's *The Scarlet Letter* provided an opportunity for in-depth exploration of motivation because Roger Chillingworth, Arthur Dimmesdale, and Hester Prynne are fully developed characters with conflicting wants and motivations. Dave's students learned that being motivated from the inside out means that we behave based on the perceptions we create, regardless of whether those perceptions are accurate or not. Shakespeare's Romeo takes his own life because he thinks that Juliet is dead. The fact that she is alive is irrelevant, because in Romeo's head, his beloved bride is gone. Students discovered that we are driven from within even when our perceptions are tragically flawed.

Weaving the ideas of internal control and motivation into his lessons helped Dave become a more effective teacher. He found it exciting to watch students argue about what motivated characters and whether their actions were responsible or irresponsible. Even though he didn't use the ideas of internal control psychology to manage disruption, Dave's students seemed appreciably more focused and attentive. He was certain this was because their discussions about internal motivation made the class more relevant and engaging.

Well before Dave began to learn about internal motivation, he had a reputation as a demanding but fair teacher. Students knew he expected a lot from them. In turn, he gave them his best—day after day, year after year. Of course, there were occasional problems, but most of Dave's students worked hard and were successful.

Addressing Students' Need for Belonging

Initially, becoming well-acquainted with internal control psychology gave Dave a frame of reference to enhance his teaching of literature. After a few months, he expanded his application of internal control psychology. He started to think about the basic needs of individual students, particularly those who were not high achievers. Megan, a student with a strong need for belonging, was Dave's first case. She was a nice kid and never intentionally disrespectful, but she frequently needed to be spoken to for off-task behavior in class—often after arriving late, something that occurred regularly.

Virtually every time Megan got into difficulty, it was related to her need for belonging. She was the quintessential social butterfly. Almost every class has one. She was late to class because she was chatting with friends. She was too social in class when Dave was attempting to teach, interfering with his need for competence. Dave knew Megan was a nice girl who would almost assuredly grow into a successful adult. She was intelligent and personable. The problem was that her need for belonging compromised her academic performance. Dave knew from conversations with his colleagues that Megan's behavior was similar in her other classes.

Dave developed a goal: to help Megan meet her need for belonging in his class by doing what he asked so she would be happy and academically productive. Dave intentionally created opportunities for Megan to utilize her strong interpersonal skills. She began to thrive. The telling point was that she no longer came to class late. Once Megan discovered, consciously or not, that she was able to satisfy her need for belonging in class, there was no compelling reason to remain in the hall. A few simple strategies helped Dave succeed with Megan and helped him use the ideas of internal motivation as a management tool and not only a way to teach literature. Specifically, Dave offered Megan the job of distributing materials for their daily lessons. This needed to be done at the beginning of class, so Megan could only do the job if she were on time. Since she got to "meet and greet" virtually every classmate as they prepared to work, she got her daily "belonging fix." As a result, Megan was able to focus and produce academically, something that she found almost impossible when Dave didn't intentionally create an environment where she could behave socially in an appropriate way.

Providing Options

Dave knew he never would have been successful if he weren't able to positively connect with his students. They knew he was demanding. They also knew he genuinely liked them and wanted them to do well. That was what made it work. Josh had a strong need for freedom and would rather fail than do what he was "made" to do. As soon as Dave provided him with options, Josh became an engaged, productive student. By helping Josh discover responsible ways to satisfy his need for autonomy, Dave became a better teacher. Dave needed to be clear about his goals and expectations. For each lesson, Dave told all students the same thing: "This is what you need to know and be able to do when we're finished. I have come up with one way for you to be successful. If you want to figure out another way that demonstrates you know what you're supposed to know and can apply the knowledge, I'm willing to consider your idea." With his strong need for autonomy, Josh thrived. He was a creative, divergent thinker, and he frequently discovered alternative ways to learn what Dave was trying to teach. For example, at the conclusion of a short story unit, Dave asked the students to write an analysis of four characters from the stories they had read. An avid musician and songwriter, Josh chose to create a compact disc of original music and lyrics depicting the conflicts, decisions, and consequences of characters from the short stories. The fact that Josh was given options diminished his need to always do things "his way." Josh's creative, divergent learning style became an asset to the class.

Fun Funneled into Productivity

Aaron had the potential to be a professional comic as an adult. Unfortunately, he was using Dave's classroom to practice. Once Dave found ways for Aaron to have fun appropriately within the classroom, Aaron toned his act down, and everyone enjoyed his creativity while simultaneously studying what needed to be learned in English class. Dave worked out an arrangement with Aaron, something that would have been impossible without a positive relationship. First, they acknowledged that they respected each other. Aaron agreed not to interfere with Dave's teaching and Dave agreed to support Aaron in his quest to find the humor in everything. The key was timing. Dave offered Aaron a couple of minutes each day for some humorous commentary. There was, however, one stipulation. Whatever Aaron discussed had to be directly related to what they were studying. Aaron had to impose structure on his creativity, something all successful artists need to do. Just like a sonnet needs to have 14 lines, Aaron needed to harness his creativity. Because he was proud of his creative humor, Aaron chose to entertain only when he had come up with something worthwhile, usually not more than once or twice a week for a couple of minutes. It was always done in a way that did not disrupt. Dave characterized Aaron's portrayal of Rip Van Winkle, waking after a 20-year slumber, as not only hilarious, but also as helping his classmates remember that landmark short story more vividly. Used judiciously, humor enhances learning, something Dave was able to incorporate into his classroom. Aaron became an asset once Dave gave him the opportunity to have fun responsibly within a classroom that maintained high academic expectations.

There were other stories from that year, all illustrating the same theme: Once Dave structured an environment where students could satisfy their needs responsibly, problematic behavior all but disappeared. Even though he didn't have many noncompliant kids, even a couple can taint a classroom, and Dave was glad he had found a way to reach more kids and enjoy his job even more.

Class Meetings Are Need-Satisfying

Another strategy that Dave found especially effective was the use of class meetings. Dave conducted brief meetings two to three times a week. Although they were only 5 to 10 minutes long, they provided an opportunity for students to feel connected, be listened to, and enjoy themselves during class. Sometimes Dave organized meetings that were content-specific, designed to reveal what students already knew about a topic that was going to be introduced. On rare occasions, Dave ran problem-solving meetings to address an issue that was keeping the class from achieving as much as possible. Most often, Dave had open meetings where students discussed issues that they found interesting. These brief meetings effectively engaged Dave's students and helped minimize disruption. By regularly having class meetings, Dave created an environment where learners could meet their needs responsibly.

The Whole Is the Sum of Its Parts, and More

About a year after he first started putting the ideas of internal motivation into practice in his classroom, Dave's district brought in a speaker for one of their professional development days. Jon Erwin, author of *The Classroom of Choice* (2004), spent the day helping teachers create classroom environments that support student achievement. The fact that Jon had been a high school English teacher made his presentation especially interesting to Dave. One thing stood out, probably because of Dave's strong interest in the basic needs. Erwin said that *classes* have needs just like individuals, and that the strength of the needs can vary dramatically from class to class. Dave immediately began to think of his own classes that year. As soon as he did, it was apparent that his 6th-period class had a strong need for belonging. They were an incredibly social group. When the lesson required them to work in cooperative groups, they did a fantastic job. They worked diligently while they interacted and they managed to stay on task.

The more Dave thought about the needs from a whole-class perspective, the more intrigued he was. Depending upon the need an activity addressed, Dave could accurately predict if the 6th-period kids were going to be successful. Dave's school operates on a rotating schedule, and it didn't matter if he met this class in the morning, just before lunch, just after lunch, or at the end of the day. They were social and driven by the belonging need all the time. Once Dave made this discovery, the solution was obvious. He structured his teaching style to match the collective learning style of the class based on their strong need for belonging. Almost immediately, on-task behavior increased and achievement improved dramatically.

Dave had another class that was much more driven by the needs for competence and freedom. For the most part, they didn't work especially well when placed in cooperative groups: Their strong need for power led to frequent conflicts. Their need for freedom led them to balk at prescribed roles and limited autonomy. Even though these students generally liked each other, they preferred to work independently most of the time. An occasional cooperative activity worked well, but too much was counterproductive. The solution? Dave identified his objective and created a lesson that was compatible with their preferred need. The "all business" class struggled when given too many cooperative activities, so Dave offered them lots of options and kept things challenging.

Dave believes students learn best when given time to process what they have been learning, creating internal meaning. With a class that is especially social, he may ask students to turn to their neighbor and take two minutes to discuss what they have been learning. If he's worried that students might drift off task, he'll have them write something first and then share for just a minute with a partner. That subtle shift works wonders. With less social, more task-oriented classes, Dave may ask them to write for several minutes. These students often learn more by processing independently. Classes with a big need for freedom might be offered a choice of writing or drawing about what they have been studying and then having the option of engaging in a one-minute conversation with a neighbor. In each case, Dave gets what he wants: students reflecting on the material they have encountered and creating meaning for themselves. By structuring activities in multiple ways, Dave has expanded the number of learners he can effectively teach.

Over time, Dave became skilled at identifying if his classes were skewed toward a particular need. Most are pretty balanced, but every year he has one or two classes that have a decided preference for one or two need areas. For every unit, Dave has developed learning activities compatible with each need area. When he has a big "belonging" class, he gives them numerous belonging activities. When he has a "freedom" class, the learning objectives remain the same, but Dave uses lots of freedom-based activities. His students are more successful because he creates an environment that matches the need profile of the class as a whole. Dave's accommodations never compromise the learning expectations. If his goal is to determine if a student has read a particular story or novel, he might be satisfied with a conversation that demonstrates that students have successfully completed the task. On the other hand, if the learning goal involves putting together a series of well-developed written paragraphs, then having a conversation about the story is not acceptable. Whatever Dave sanctions appropriately addresses his objectives.

Dave has been intentionally constructing his classroom based on the need-strength of the group for some time now. Some of his colleagues have told him that they think he is "giving in" by teaching to match the need-strength of his classes. "Part of growing up is learning how to adapt to the demands of the environment," they tell him. "The world doesn't adapt for us. We thrive when we learn to adapt to the environment." When confronted by their reasoning, Dave reminds himself that these colleagues are looking at things from an external orientation. As someone committed to internal motivation, Dave takes an inside-out approach. He asks himself what *he* wants as a teacher. He is the teacher he wants to be when he creates a need-satisfying environment. He doesn't think he's "giving in" to his students. "It's not a competition. It's a cooperative venture," he says. Of course, classes where power and freedom are the dominant needs sometimes include students with a high need for belonging, just as classes characterized by a high need for connecting typically have a few students who are less social and who work better independently. Individualizing lessons and providing differentiated instruction allows Dave to structure learning environments that are need-satisfying for all students in his classes.

Dave's approach, based on fostering and nurturing internal motivation and the desire to succeed academically, allows his students to be more successful. As a teacher, that's what matters to him. By intentionally giving his classes, as well as individual students, what they need, he is a better teacher.

Commentary

Dave initially applied internal control psychology to his teaching of literature. Discussing the internal pictures of characters in literature and the needs that drive them represents a natural application of internal control psychology in the classroom. Students in history classes can study historical figures using the same process. In fact, you can apply internal control psychology to any subject that involves human interaction and competing goals.

As Dave became more familiar with internal control psychology, he began to consider the unwanted behavior that occasionally compromised his classroom. Knowing that all behavior is purposeful and designed to satisfy needs, Dave set about discovering what need was being met by disruptive behavior. He then created opportunities for his students to meet their needs by participating in activities he sanctioned and that enhanced learning. Soon Dave had virtually eliminated unwanted behavior, and his students were both happier and more academically productive.

Classes, like individual students, differ in terms of need-strength. Dave found that some classes need more connections, some need more freedom, and some are more driven by pure achievement. He structured his teaching to match the style of each class. While he delivered the same content and maintained the same expectations, Dave developed flexible ways to teach that matched the need profile of each class. By developing flexibility, Dave added a creative dimension to his teaching style that helped him be more successful with more classes. And by attending to the specific need-strengths of individual students, he maximized the chances of all students being involved and productive in his classroom.

What You Can Do

• If you teach a subject that involves human interaction like English or social studies, discuss the internal pictures and drives of the characters with your students. These discussions will help the characters seem more "real," and the students will become more engaged in learning.

• Pay attention to the strength of your students' needs. In most classrooms, there are a few students who have especially strong needs in one or two areas. Find ways to help them satisfy their needs by doing what you ask. They will be less disruptive and more academically productive.

• Consider your class as a whole and determine if it has a particular need area that is especially strong. Deliver instruction to match the style and "personality" of your class, regardless of whether it is more belonging-driven, freedom-driven, or competence-driven. When your instruction matches what the class needs, they will be more engaged and more productive.

• Conduct class meetings frequently. Meetings can be brief. They can focus on academic content, problematic behavior, or issues of interest. Class meetings are need-satisfying because students feel connected, listened to, and free.

• Match your teaching to the style of the class. Higher standards are more likely to be achieved when you provide instruction that is compatible with the personality of your learners.

Chapter 12

From Telling to Asking

When I told Ann I was putting together stories of people using internal control psychology and asked her if she'd be willing to be included, she agreed in an instant.

"As a high school guidance counselor, what's different now that you intentionally work with the ideas of internal motivation in mind?" I asked. "People need a sense of how it *looks different in action* to become interested in learning about internal control psychology."

"Can't blame them for that," Ann said. "Most of us are too busy to learn something that has no real-life value."

Ann is a high school counselor with over 30 years' experience. She had seen ideas come and go, and she is not above speaking her mind frankly and forcefully. It was especially interesting to talk with Ann because her knowledge of internal control psychology is based on reading she has done and conversation with a friend who is particularly well-versed in the theory.

"Ann," I said, "you provide an important perspective for this project. You have qualities that will make you credible to a lot of readers."

"You mean I'm old," she said. Ann's smile and tone of voice clearly signaled that she was not offended. She is a woman who is comfortable with who she is and likes being acknowledged as the veteran she is.

"I mean you've been around long enough not to be fooled easily. Just as importantly, you've never attended any workshops about internal control psychology. I want people to see these concepts as accessible, not something that requires extensive, formal training to use."

"Then I guess I'm about the best person you could have picked to talk with. I have never attended any workshop specifically about internal control psychology. I've never had a course that was focused exclusively on internal control. I've read things by Glasser and Alfie Kohn and picked up other information in journals I read regularly. I have a reasonable grasp of the concepts, but I'm no expert. What I have learned, I like."

"Would you consider yourself a practitioner of internal control psychology?" I asked.

Ann laughed. "I would never think to ask myself that question. I can see why that might be interesting to you, but it has no meaning for me. I just call myself a high school counselor."

"Ann, since you've become familiar with internal control psychology, what's different about how you work with kids?"

"That's easy," she said. "I have moved from being a 'teller' to an 'asker.' That's the single most important change in my counseling. Other things haven't changed at all."

"Like what?" I asked.

"Putting an emphasis on relationships. I've been doing that for more than 30 years. Different theorists have called it different things. The name doesn't matter. What matters is that a counselor needs to make connections with their counselees. Without that connection, you're sunk. With it, you can move mountains."

"So the emphasis on relationships is something you agree with, even though you didn't 'get it' from internal control psychology? Is that right?"

"Exactly," Ann replied. "Glasser talks about involvement and relationships. Rogers talks about unconditional positive regard. Everyone calls it something. It boils down to remembering that you are a human being helping another human being. I knew that was essential before I ever heard of internal control psychology."

"Tell me how you changed from telling to asking," I said.

"I was having dinner with a couple of friends, including Gloria, my friend who's well-versed in internal control psychology. I mentioned that my nickname at school was 'Mom.' It started because I used to tell the kids, 'You've got your mother at home. I'm your mom here. I'll tell you what to do. Just trust your mother, do what I say, and you'll be just fine.'

"I loved the role of surrogate mom. I told students what to do. I gave advice. All day. Every day. For years. By the way, it was good advice. I can't think of much that I told a kid to do that I regret. It wasn't the *content* of my comments. It was the fact that I *told* them what to do instead of helping them figure out on their own what they wanted and needed to do."

"That sounds like a major shift, Ann," I said. "What led you to change?"

"I know that at least two important factors were part of the change. One seems simple. It was paying attention to the looks on the faces of the kids as I told them what to do, as I *insisted* on what they do. Some looked angry, like they were offended that I was telling them what to do, even though it was *good stuff* I was prescribing. Some looked bored, like they had heard countless versions of this before and they simply wanted to get it over with as quickly as possible. Some looked relieved, like there was someone there to rescue them because they were uncertain about what direction they wanted to take their life. But guess what I never saw?"

"What's that, Ann?"

"I never saw joy. By prescribing, I never helped kids discover anything on their own. I was so busy orchestrating that I never helped them develop the ability to grow up. At the time, I thought I was making their lives easier by telling them what to do. I was older, more experienced, and had enough distance to look at things more objectively. Now I think that I delayed the growing up we all have to do. It was the absence of joy in their eyes that clued me in."

"Ann, you said there were at least two factors. Other than the absence of happiness on the faces and in the eyes of the kids, what was there?"

"The second thing came from two sources, a student and my friend Gloria. It was like a one-two punch. I was working with Chad, a junior in high school. As always, I was telling him what he should do. I was full of my usual good advice. When I used my famous 'I'm your mom here at school' line, Chad said to me, 'I already have a mother. I have someone who loves me and who constantly tells me what to do. I don't need another mother. I need someone to help me figure out what *I* want to do with my life.'"

"That must have been quite a wake-up call," I said.

"I wish it were," Ann replied. "In fact, I somehow managed to deflect Chad's comment and continued to tell him what was best for him. But I got lucky. I had dinner with Gloria that night and I mentioned my meeting with Chad. Gloria asked, 'Do you think maybe he's right?'

"I had never questioned if there was anything wrong with being the advice-dispensing counselor I had been for years. No one had ever complained. I had always received positive evaluations. I had come to believe that as adults it was our *job* to tell kids what they should do. Gloria's question came at just the right time. I acknowledged that I told instead of asked. As a counselor, that's not what I wanted to do, and from that day on, everything changed."

"Ann, I'd like you to tell me *exactly* how things changed after that day. What looked or sounded different from before? I can appreciate the internal shift you experienced, but I'd like a clear picture of how that was expressed differently in your counseling. Is that something you can put words to?"

"Sure. Let me use one example that is typical of what I do regularly as a high school counselor. As I would talk to kids, say a junior in high school, I would simply assume that if they were a good student that they wanted to go to college. I'd say things like, 'Have you figured out what colleges interest you?' without even considering that the student may not be interested in college at this time. When someone asks you if you have thought about *which* colleges interest you, the whole question of *if college inter-ests you* has been taken off the table. Once the student identified a few *appropriate possibilities*—and I made sure to direct the conversation in such a way that they picked schools that I would approve of—then I told them what they needed to do in order to maximize their chances of getting in. Once I determined that I wanted to be a *counselor* instead of a director, I began asking lots of questions."

"Like?"

"Like 'Have you given any thought about what you want to do after graduation?' 'What do see yourself doing in five years?' 'Do you think you'll be living in this area or do you see yourself moving away?' Questions that didn't have an implied *right answer.* Questions that invited kids to think and express themselves. Questions that invited them to grow and take ownership of their lives."

"It seems like you gave up a lot of the control that you had so successfully wielded for so long," I said. "Was that difficult?"

"I was petrified at first. I think you've identified the heart of the matter. Before, I had orchestrated things. There were exceptions from time to time, but for the most part, I was in control. Initially, this was scary."

"But you kept at it, obviously," I said.

"Interestingly, it wasn't that hard. The fear was all in my head. The places the kids went when I gave them more freedom and control were almost always where I would have taken them anyway. I remembered reading years ago that kids generally hold the same long-term values as their parents. They may argue about music and clothing and hair style—all the short-term stuff. But they tend to be more like their parents than different about the big stuff. I used to be the director. Now I was the facilitator. Ironically, we ended up in the same place. The difference was that the students had greater control. They didn't feel manipulated. The joy I had not seen before was splashed across their faces.

"I remember one girl in particular, probably because she was able to articulate what so many others were thinking. After we had finished talking about what she wanted, she got this wonderful grin on her face. 'It's so weird,' she said. 'I always thought that I wanted to go to college and get a good job because it was something that my parents expected. I've just realized that it's what I want for myself. Even though I'll be doing the same thing, I know I'm doing it for me, not for them.' That's when I knew that asking, not telling, was the key to effective counseling."

"Did things always go smoothly?" I asked.

"Of course not," Ann said. "I continue to have my challenges. One question really helps me assess the students' level of motivation. Now I universally ask, 'How much do you want this? Enough to talk about it, or do you want it enough to *really work* for it?'"

"And that's successful?" I asked.

"It's like magic," Ann answered. "It doesn't even matter what they say."

"That's interesting," I said. "Tell me what you mean."

"When a kid really wants something and is committed to working for it, it almost always plays out pretty easily. Sometimes I have to help them, but more often than not, they're successful on their own when they have a clear picture and strong motivation."

"I've got that part," I countered. "But what about the kids who aren't that motivated?"

"I have discovered that asking helps kids figure out how much they *really* want something. Often, they discover that *they* don't want something nearly as much as someone else—usually their parents—wants it for them." Ann paused. "And sometimes they discover that they want something but they lack the motivation to get it."

"Explain that for me, Ann," I said.

"Sure," Ann said. "Checking out the intensity of motivation has been very helpful to me. Lots of us want things *as long as we don't have to work very hard to get them!* For example, if you asked me if I wanted to have lots of money, I would say, 'Yes.' But I'm not willing to work a lot more to actually *be* rich. I want it, yes. I just don't want to work very hard to get it."

"Explain how this relates to school," I said to Ann.

"Lots of kids want to do well," she said. "Too many of them aren't willing to do the work necessary to be successful. I now help kids not only identify their wants but also assess their level of motivation."

"What does that look like?" I asked.

"I begin by asking my students if they are willing to do the work necessary to be successful. If they say, 'Yes,' then I move into the planning phase."

"But if they say, 'No'?"

"I don't accept their answer at face value. I ask them to imagine being successful and ask them if they are happier when they consider that hypothetical outcome. Very often, visualizing future success helps students create the motivation to get started. Visualization can strengthen a want and generate the motivation necessary to achieve. It's a powerful counseling tool."

"How has this worked?" I asked.

"Wonderfully," answered Ann. "The past year has been the most rewarding of my career. I have become the facilitator I wanted to be when I started this job. I am comfortable when kids are not motivated to go where I would have directed them. At the same time, I work with lots of kids who are adequately motivated but lack the behaviors necessary to be successful. Now that I have figured out how to distinguish between the two, I can be more helpful to them. If they are adequately motivated but don't know how to succeed, I help them expand their behavioral arsenal. It's much more rewarding than the prescribing I used to do."

"Would you like to add anything else, Ann?" I asked.

"Only that I spent more years than I wanted to in the role of 'mom.' I now function as a facilitator and guide. It's more fulfilling, and I am helping kids more. As I wind down my career, I am glad to know that I will end up *asking* more than *telling*. That's something all good counselors do."

Commentary

Ann discussed the importance of building a positive relationship with her counselees, saying, "Without that connection, you're sunk. With it, you can move mountains." Even though Ann did not learn internal control psychology until later in her career, she had always put a special emphasis on developing a strong connection with her students. That strong foundation was the cornerstone of her success.

Ann learned the importance of asking questions rather than telling her counselees what to do. Her training had probably included classes called something like "Behavioral Analysis and Prescription." She had been taught to be prescriptive. Doling out advice, even sound advice, is fraught with problems. If students do what you suggest and things go poorly, they typically blame you. When things go well, students become increasingly dependent. In both cases, students miss the opportunity to develop responsibility.

When Ann switched from telling to asking, she helped her counselees practice decision making and acting responsibly. An experienced counselor, Ann asked questions that led to helpful self-evaluation. She gave up the role of "expert" and took on the more satisfying role of "facilitator." Like Ben in Chapter 8, Ann helped clarify the lines of responsibility. Her job was to guide her students. Their job was to own their decisions and their lives.

One thing I emphasize in my work with educators is getting a clear definition of our roles and responsibilities. Despite her good intentions, when Ann took on the parental role, she compromised her ability to be an effective counselor. When she focused on counseling and guiding, she became more effective and more satisfied professionally.

Ann helped students assess their level of motivation. This practice is important. It is not enough to ask students if they want something. They need to be asked *how much* they want something and *how much effort* they are willing to put forth to be successful. The skilled counselor helps students identify the strength of their motivation. Ann had students engage in visualization. This powerful strategy can jump-start students who lack adequate motivation to succeed. Visualization helps create the internal picture that will lead to the motivation necessary for success. Ann used this strategy to initiate the change process with students whose level of motivation was suspect.

What You Can Do

• Above all, foster a positive relationship with your counselees.

• Define your role and responsibilities.

• As much as possible, stop giving advice and telling students what they should do. Even if you give good advice, this practice does not help students become responsible decision makers.

• Ask your counselees questions that facilitate self-evaluation. Have them identify what they want and explore what behavioral options will help them achieve their goals.

• Challenge students by asking questions that assess their level of motivation. Are they motivated enough merely to talk with you in an office, or are they motivated enough to really make themselves successful?

• Use visualization with students who seem to lack the motivation to take effective action. Often, when students visualize the positive outcomes they want, they become adequately energized.

Chapter 13

From Enforcing to Teaching Responsibility and Fostering Positive Relationships

Steve is a high school vice principal studying and applying the ideas of internal control psychology in virtual isolation. He characterizes his building principal as "supportive," but notes that she is neither well-acquainted with the concepts nor interested in implementing them throughout the school. No other staff in his school of about 800 students from grades 9–12 have had any training either. Steve is truly a lone wolf, someone committed to the notion of motivation from the inside out while working with teachers who use the usual rewards and punishment.

It's rare to encounter a situation like Steve's. Typically, a principal initiates training for the staff, or classroom teachers enroll in a workshop and bring the ideas back to their colleagues. It's unusual for a secondary school vice principal to be the only person studying internal control psychology within a school. Curious, I asked Steve how he became interested in the area of internal motivation.

Steve said, "Initially, I hoped it would improve discipline. As a high school VP, I'm the guy who handles most of the behavioral infractions. I'm always on the lookout for strategies that will make my life easier and my job less tedious."

There is considerable research showing that behavior improves when internal control psychology is applied, but the focus is usually on creating need-satisfying environments for both staff and students, because disruptive behavior is less likely to occur in those settings. When discipline is discussed by those who practice internal control psychology, it is generally couched in terms of self-discipline.

Ron, the middle school principal introduced in Chapter 9, is an example of someone who has created an environment where there is no reason to behave poorly. I wondered if Steve was seeking the magic pill that would eliminate unwanted behavior in school without changing school climate and the relationships within the building. "What do you think now, Steve?"

"I guess I've done a complete 180 since I started this journey a few years ago," Steve answered. "It was clear from the outset that we weren't going to talk about discipline, at least not in the reward/punishment sense. But a few things impressed me, and I decided this training would be valuable."

"What got your interest?" I asked.

"The two things that impressed me most were the idea that all behavior is purposeful and that everyone is doing the best they can. As the VP, I'm constantly dealing with all the annoying infractions that characterize most high schools. Suddenly it all made sense. All behavior is purposeful. Kids who are behaving poorly aren't doing it for no reason. We don't sanction what they're doing. It's not OK. But it's purposeful. The other idea was that everyone is doing the best they can. At first I had difficulty with this. All day long I work with kids who are in trouble, and I was being told that they were doing the best they can? It didn't square with my view of how people behave. But the concept was explained more fully, that people are doing the best they can, *given the resources they have available at the time*. It gave me a new way to do deal with kids."

"Can you explain?" I asked.

"Previously, when a kid was sent to me for violating some school regulation, I was the enforcer. I treated kids well, but simply imposed the consequences stipulated in the student handbook. Nothing more and nothing less. Now, I operate as a *teacher*, not just an *enforcer*. I still enforce the rules. I still invoke the sanctions. I'm not about to undermine the school. At the same time,

I have moved beyond the enforcer-only role I had taken on. Now I teach kids how to behave in ways that we endorse. I've put it together with the idea that all behavior is purposeful, and I have a more satisfying way to do my job."

"Explain what's different, Steve, if you will."

"Sure. I remember when it came together for me. Russell had just been in a fight. The school policy called for an out-of-school suspension. I had been down this road numerous times with kids, and I always fell back on the rules, enforcing them with as little emotion as possible, hoping that the suspension would keep the kid from misbehaving again. Sometimes it worked, sometimes it didn't. With Russell, I decided to try something different. I told him that I heard he had been in a fight. He admitted it freely. I then told him that he would be suspended from school. I wanted him to know that the conversation we were about to have wouldn't change the consequence that was stipulated in the student handbook. I then said, 'Russ, I'm wondering why you decided to fight. You know we don't allow fighting in school, but you must have had a reason for doing what you did. No matter what you tell me, it won't change the suspension, but I'd still like to know why you did it.' Russell was more than willing to talk, saying, 'This kid has been bothering my cousin for a few weeks. I told him to stop, but he didn't, so I hit him.' I said, 'So is your family important to you?' 'Absolutely,' he replied. 'What about friendship and loyalty?' 'Same thing. Very important,' Russell said. 'So if you could figure out how to be a good friend, care about your family, and be loyal, would that be worth knowing?' I asked. 'You can't do that!' Russell said. 'That doesn't answer my question, Russ,' I said. 'I just want to know if it would be worth learning how to be a good friend, someone who is loyal, and someone who cares about his family—without getting into fights and breaking school rules.' Russell looked confused, but said, 'Well, yeah. I just don't know how to do it.' 'I've got great news for you, Russell. I can help you. When you return to school, let's talk.' At that moment I switched from being an enforcer to being a teacher. I've never looked back."

"Steve," I said, "you have begun to counsel using the idea

that we're internally motivated when you encounter disciplinary infractions. Kids typically like to blame others and tell us how they 'had to' do something or someone 'made' them do it. It sounds as if you're turning things upside down. Is that right?"

"All the time," Steve answered. "And I'm having a positive impact on quite a few kids. I have been careful to work closely with the counselors so they don't think I'm trying to step on their toes. And teachers want to be supported by administration. But I'm teaching and helping kids take responsibility."

"You began learning about internal control psychology to improve student behavior. Has it helped in other areas as well?" I asked.

"I thought about all the things that could be better in our school, and in every case it seemed like a big part of the difficulty involved the quality of the relationships we had."

"So what did you do?"

"First, you've got to know something about high school. Teachers are feeling increasingly under attack, and there are more demands, many which take away from what brought teachers to the profession in the first place. Most teachers entered the profession because they love kids and want to help them grow into successful adults. The definition of 'successful adult' has become increasingly narrow and has been determined by non-educators. Now teachers are required to administer high-stakes tests, many which have little to do with how successful kids will become, either academically or more generally. Regardless of the validity of these tests, if teachers don't prepare kids to do well, their jobs are in jeopardy. Beyond that, there are all the requirements of No Child Left Behind. Teachers are understandably pre-occupied with demonstrating they are 'highly qualified' even if that means they are less effective! My point is simply that teachers are increasingly stressed. Especially in high schools, the emphasis is on subject-area expertise. With that in mind, there were not many places I could have an impact on the school, at least as it is currently organized."

"You mentioned relationships," I offered.

"Yeah. I remember hearing someone cite a study about how

well high school teachers knew the kids in their school. In this study, teachers were asked to simply indicate if they knew a student. According to the speaker I listened to, 40 percent of the kids were identified as being known by *no staff member in the school*! I'll admit that this astounded me, and I'm not even sure if it was accurate, but it got me thinking. I wondered how many of our teachers knew kids who might not be in their classes. If a kid isn't in one of our classes, we're often unaware of who that kid is."

"What did you do to strengthen relationships within a traditional high school?"

"I'm involved in scheduling for the building. I asked a few teachers what they talked about during their prep period or during lunch. I wasn't surprised to hear that most of them never talked about specific students. They discussed what they were doing for the weekend, family issues, things in the news, that sort of thing. Occasionally, two teachers in the same department might discuss something related to the curriculum. But they never discussed kids."

"Why not?" I asked.

"It's a function of the typical high school schedule. Two teachers might share a small percentage of students, but for the most part, your student rosters are very different from mine. It makes no sense for you and me to discuss individual students. If we were going to discuss professional issues, it would likely be about something that has an impact on the two of us, like if we were in the same department. We almost always have class rosters with little overlap. We're more likely to talk about the weather. At least that's something we have in common."

"How did you counteract this, Steve?"

"I implemented three things that didn't affect any teachers directly, but which had the potential to change the culture of the school. First, I instituted a system where teachers kept the same homeroom for all four years kids were in the high school. Previously, kids changed homerooms every year. I kept them in the same room all four years."

"How did that help?"

"It meant that each homeroom teacher got to know kids over an extended period of time, even if they never had the kid in class. We've only been doing it for a couple of years, but already teachers are telling me how much they enjoy watching the kids mature over time.

"A second thing I did was introduce our Connections program."

"What's that?" I asked.

"I had our guidance counselors identify kids who they thought would benefit from positive adult attention every day. These are kids who might not need to see the counselor on a regular basis, but they are the kids who might slip through the cracks or the kids who might do poorly if they don't know that some adult in the school really cares about them."

"How does Connections work?"

"It's completely voluntary. Initially, only a few teachers participated. Now, the majority do."

"Are you asking the teachers to counsel kids?" I asked.

"Absolutely not!" exclaimed Steve. "The sole objective is to connect with these kids. You are not counseling, personally or academically. In fact, I suggest to teachers that they don't even mention anything academic unless the student really wants to discuss academics. We only ask that they connect with the student each day by saying 'hello' and asking what's going on, what plans the kid has for the weekend, and so on. These kids are already in your homeroom. It's not time-intensive. It's intentionally low-tech."

"You make it sound almost simplistic. What's the purpose?" I asked.

Steve answered, "There is considerable research that suggests kids who are better connected do better academically and behave more appropriately. I figured this was a way for us to do something easy that couldn't hurt and would probably help."

"Has it helped?"

"Absolutely," Steve said. "I track the number of referrals I receive for inappropriate behavior, and the numbers have dropped dramatically the past two years. Kids who feel a connection are less likely to act out. At the same time, our kids are doing better on state-mandated tests."

"So you now keep kids with one homeroom teacher for four years and you have introduced the Connections program. Have you done anything else to improve relationships?" I asked.

"Most high schools run on a matrix schedule, and teachers don't have common caseloads. I wanted to change that without completely disrupting the way our schedule runs, so I created unofficial teaching partnerships."

"How does that work?" I asked.

"I paired English and social studies teachers together and math and science teachers together. Let's pretend you and I are a team, and I'm the English teacher. I get my students and you, as the social studies teacher, get the same kids. The kids may not be together in class, but everyone who has me for English will have you for social studies. And you and I will have the same prep time. This makes it easy and natural for us to talk and plan together. The same system is used for the math and science partners."

"Why didn't you just extend it to all four subjects and have academic teams like many middle schools have?"

"For one thing, it would have compromised some of the scheduling flexibility we currently enjoy. Plus, a high school is different from a middle school, and we want to preserve that difference. Having loosely defined mini-teams suits us well."

"What are the advantages from the relationship standpoint?" I asked.

"There are two primary benefits," Steve said. "First, because you and I share the same students, we are more likely to have conversations about kids. We naturally will talk about which kids are doing well, which ones are struggling, what things we're studying. It naturally facilitates professional conversation about kids. Second, we've found that teachers plan more carefully now. If I know that you are giving a major test on Thursday, I'm likely to avoid overloading the kids and may even scale back on homework the night before. Kids are doing as much work, but teachers are more respectful of their partners than when they worked in relative isolation."

"Anything else?"

"We have more interdisciplinary teaching than in the past. As I said before, the state and federal mandates keep teachers pretty locked into their subject areas, but anything that helps kids see the interconnectedness among subject areas is helpful. A few of our teaching partners have put together units that tie subjects together nicely. From the relationship perspective, this has helped create stronger connections among staff and has helped break down some subject-area boundaries found in typical high schools."

"Steve, it seems as if you have been able to implement some important changes in your school. Do you think your school is ready to embrace internal control psychology?"

"I don't know. Our school remains traditional in lots of ways. At first, that bothered me, but my wife helped me see that being upset was a choice I was making. Since I had no plans to leave the school and the school wasn't likely to undergo dramatic change, I could either choose to be miserable or I could do something to improve things in ways that didn't upset people too much. I chose to do my small part."

Steve's unassuming and self-effacing style belies the fact that he has been a catalyst for important change within his building. Steve's story demonstrates that effective changes can be implemented even by those working in relative isolation. Steve works in a traditional high school, with a traditional principal, and has no colleagues joining him in his attempts to apply the concepts of internal control psychology. By expanding his role from "enforcer" to "teacher," Steve derives greater satisfaction from his role. And by structuring the schedule to foster positive relationships, Steve has helped decrease disruption and increase student achievement. As a result of his initiatives, teachers are collaborating more and providing more interdisciplinary experiences for kids, while still functioning within a traditional high school faced with all the external pressures brought on by state and federal mandates. Steve may say he is taking small steps, but in fact, he has done much to improve his school.

Commentary

Steve was first attracted to internal control psychology because he thought it would improve discipline within his school. In that regard, his story is fairly common. Even though most practitioners of internal control psychology focus on creating a need-satisfying learning environment that fosters self-discipline, many educators are initially interested in how to effectively manage disruption. Steve found that he could do much more than be an effective disciplinarian if he began to apply the principles of internal control psychology.

Steve learned that *all* behavior, even inappropriate behavior, is purposeful. That concept allowed Steve to move from being someone who simply enforced rules to a person who continued to teach while he functioned as an administrator. As Steve explored with students the purpose behind their inappropriate behavior, he helped them develop responsible, prosocial behaviors to meet their needs. Most administrators will tell you that they miss teaching. With the help of internal control psychology, Steve expanded his role and became an effective teacher of at-risk students.

Steve's development of the Connections program underscores the importance of building and maintaining positive relationships with students. Even though adolescents are driven by power and autonomy, they still need to feel a sense of connection to their peers and their school. Research repeatedly suggests that students who feel connected are less likely to act out aggressively. Connections is a simple program that ameliorates the feelings of alienation and isolation that plague too many secondary schools.

The creation of mini-teams builds a sense of community within a school. Increasingly, larger schools are seeing the wisdom of creating small learning teams and communities. The mini-teams that Steve created did more than foster a sense of community among the students. Just as importantly, they built connections among staff members and between departments. With a focus on distinct academic disciplines, it is easy for secondary teachers to forget that learning is fundamentally an interdisciplinary adventure. Steve's mini-teams broke down unnecessary barriers and led to more interdisciplinary teaching.

What You Can Do

• Remember that you are, above all, a teacher. Be certain that your role always supports learning. Effective discipline involves good teaching.

• Remember that all behavior is purposeful. When students figure out how to meet their needs with appropriate behavior, inappropriate behavior will diminish. There is no reason to behave badly in a need-satisfying environment.

• Build and maintain positive relationships. You can only effectively teach students with whom you have developed a positive relationship. This is especially true with students who violate school rules. Connected kids are less likely to act out aggressively and engage in acts of violence. The best violence prevention program is to build a sense of community.

• If you work in a large school, find ways to shrink it.

• Remember that learning is an interdisciplinary experience. Encourage teachers to break down artificial barriers between subjects and offer as many interdisciplinary experiences to students as possible. Students and teachers alike will be energized.

Chapter 14

Reflections of a High School Senior

Matt is a serious, articulate young man, a high school senior preparing for graduation. Many of his teachers have used internal control psychology, something Matt believes has prepared him for college. I asked Matt to identify what has been most helpful and meaningful.

"There is no doubt that the single most beneficial thing for me was the Competence-Based Classroom," Matt said. "I was fortunate to have a couple of teachers who used this approach in the 9th grade. The CBC was critically important to my development as a student, especially in the 9th grade. The teachers who used this approach told us from the first day of class that they believed in our ability and that they would only accept work that was *B* or better. In one of those classes, World History, it was no big deal. I liked the class and found it pretty easy. Even though the teacher insisted that I redo a few papers and a couple of tests to demonstrate competence, I easily earned a *B* or *A* every term."

"What about the other class?" I asked.

"Math was different. I had been placed in an advanced math class as a freshman because I had done well in middle school. However, I wasn't especially good in math. I had done well in middle school because I always did my homework, earned extra points because I stayed after for extra help before tests, and participated actively in class. I had been an *A* student in math in middle school, but I wasn't very good at it.

"My freshman-year math teacher told us all that we were going to earn an *A* or *B* and that we would be given as much time as we needed. I soon learned that this class was a killer and I was just looking for a *C*. I even told the teacher that I was comfortable with a *C*. He told me that if I was in his class, he assumed I could do the work and I was expected to earn a *B* or better, just like everybody else."

"Did this motivate you to work harder?" I asked.

"At first, I figured he was testing me and I worked hard enough to get a *C*. At least I thought I did. I completed the homework, participated in class, and was a cooperative student. I just didn't do very well on the tests and quizzes. When report cards were issued, I received no grade in math. I thought there had been a mistake. There wasn't. My teacher told me that my report card would stay blank until I earned the *B* he knew I could get!

"I thought he was just kidding, but he assured me that I had to earn a *B* or better or repeat the class. I told him that I wasn't good in math and just wanted to get a *C* by doing my homework and being a nice kid. He told me he was glad I was a nice kid but that was 'an irrelevance' to him. He wanted competence and wouldn't settle for anything less."

"It sounds like he was fairly tough," I said. "Is that accurate?"

"I wouldn't say that," answered Matt. "He was willing to help any student who was having difficulty. The one thing he wouldn't accept was a student doing less than *B* work. It was hard, but I ended up earning a *B* in math and probably learned more in that class than in any other class I ever took. I still don't like math, but this teacher taught me more because he believed in me as a student and insisted I perform. It wasn't enough to be cooperative and do the homework—I needed to perform. But he was there all year for me to help me achieve. I'm more proud of that *B* than any other grade I received in high school. I know I worked hard for this teacher because he not only believed in my ability, he really likes kids. He never eased up, but he showed every day that he really cared about all of his students."

"You sound like you are an advocate of the Competence-Based Classroom," I said.

Matt nodded in agreement and said, "I think the Competence-Based Classroom should be used in every class in freshman and sophomore year. I would have happily settled for a *C* in math. I know lots of kids who would have been happy just to pass freshman and sophomore year. You don't know at that time that grades you are getting have an impact on your future. I'm planning on going to a good four-year college. If I didn't do so well in math as a freshman, I might not have been accepted into some colleges that have accepted me. The CBC makes sure that every student succeeds. I think that's especially important for freshmen and sophomores. Most 9th and 10th grade students aren't thinking much about their future. They can blow off a subject, hurt themselves, and not even realize it until it's too late. The CBC helps kids do well until they're a little older and able to make better decisions for themselves. Once I became a junior, I was more focused on getting into a good college and had a better understanding of what I needed to do in order to get there."

"What other things stand out as being especially helpful to you, Matt?" I asked.

"Knowing that my teachers cared about me and knew who I was. It's pretty easy to be invisible in high school. Teachers only see you for a class period, and they're so focused on their subject that it's easy for them to not know you as a person. The teachers I will remember are the ones who took the time to know a little bit about me, who asked me how my weekend was, who asked about what I was doing. Because of how those teachers treated me, I ended up liking their classes more, learning more, and maybe even wanting to study that subject in college. High school teachers don't know how much their students appreciate it when we're recognized as real people.

"The other thing that means a lot to every kid is to be respected. The teachers I admire the most are the ones who respect all the students, even the ones who act like jerks. It's not a big deal to treat good students with respect, but a teacher who treats wise guys with respect really earns my admiration. I had one teacher who had a poster in her room that said, 'Respect isn't a gift. You have to earn it.' I always thought that was the most ridiculous poster I'd ever seen. What's special about respecting someone who's 'earned it'? I want to be a person who treats others with respect no matter how I'm treated. If I only respect those who respect me, I'm letting other people control me. You might disrespect me, but you can never make me a disrespectful person. That's what internal motivation is all about."

Matt was a young man with strong opinions. I asked him if he had anything else to add.

"I liked it when my teachers explained to us why it was important to learn what they were teaching. A lot of times it's not real obvious why we have to learn things in our classes. At least it's not obvious to most students. When teachers tell us we need to learn it because 'it's on the test' or 'it's part of the state competency exams,' it's a real turnoff. It's like they don't know why their own subject is worth learning except that it's on some test. When teachers help us see how to use what they're teaching, it makes it much easier to get excited about learning. I know it takes time to explain why learning is important, but students end up learning more when teachers explain why studying something is worthwhile.

"I feel like I got a good education and my teachers prepared me for college. The things that were most important were the Competence-Based Classroom, having teachers who got to know the students as people, having teachers who respected their students, and having teachers who explained how to use what we were learning in the real world. I think if all teachers did these things, high school would be even better for more students."

Commentary

Matt makes a compelling argument about the value of the Competence-Based Classroom for freshmen and sophomores. He suggests that our traditional system allows ill-equipped students to make decisions that have important consequences. Matt favors limiting freedom by insisting on high-quality work until students are more prepared to make choices with lifelong consequences. Our traditional system provides students with more freedom, but giving students freedom when they lack responsible behaviors is setting some of them up for failure.

Matt is quick to point out that his math teacher regularly demonstrated that he liked his students and had confidence in them. The demanding nature of the Competence-Based Classroom requires a strong teacher-student relationship. Teachers who are academically demanding but don't build a strong connection with their students will not succeed. Matt was willing to work hard and overcome his weakness in math because he knew his demanding teacher believed in him and liked him. Students are not looking for teachers who are easy. They are looking for teachers who bring out the best in them, something that requires a strong relationship.

As Matt says, it is "easy to be invisible in high school." He appreciated those teachers who got to know him as a human being, not just a student. We sometimes think that high school students want to disconnect from adults. While high school students cherish their autonomy, they value being recognized by important adults in their lives, including their teachers.

Like every student, Matt wanted to be respected. In my career of over 30 years, adolescents who dislike school repeatedly mention feeling disrespected and not listened to. When adolescents believe they are listened to and respected, they put forth a strong effort as long as they believe they have a reasonable chance of being successful.

Finally, Matt emphasized the importance of relevance. Unskilled teachers do not adequately explain the usefulness of what is being taught. They take it for granted that students understand the relevance of the lesson and will work hard. Unless students have an especially strong connection with the teacher, they will only do their best work when they fully understand why it is important. Effective teachers provide specific examples of how learning can be applied by students in a way that is relevant to them. Once students see the relevance of what they are asked to do, their natural internal motivation leads them to do higher-quality academic work.

What You Can Do

- Remember that high school students want to feel connected to their teachers and their school. Even students who adopt an air of indifference want to feel a sense of community and connection. Make it easy for the students to feel a sense of belonging in your school.

- Let your students know you have confidence in their ability to do high-quality academic work. Especially if you offer a challenging experience (like the Competence-Based Classroom), students need to know you believe in them. Your confidence can inspire them to do work they didn't think they could do.

- If you want to be a respectful adult, give respect unconditionally, even to those who haven't earned it. Students will respect you even more when you respect everyone. When you respect others, you help them satisfy their need for power and they will perform better for you.

- Be sure to help students see the relevance of what you ask them to learn. The question "Why do we have to learn this?" is an opportunity to explain the importance of what you are teaching.

Final Thoughts

Student motivation is the most important issue in education today. Although teachers are underpaid and class size is increasing, a room full of highly motivated students achieves admirably. We just have to figure how to increase student motivation. The sad truth is that too few students work to their potential. Until more students decide to work harder, there will be no significant improvement in our schools no matter how much better we teach.

Most professional development initiatives are aimed at enhancing instruction and strengthening curriculum. In recent years, our ability to instruct has improved substantially. There is greater consistency in what we teach. We deliver content better now than at any other time in our history. Curriculum and instruction represent only one half of the equation, however. Higher standards, a well-designed curriculum, and exemplary instruction are of limited value unless students are engaged and motivated to learn what is being taught.

Until now, we have relied on external control psychology, attempting to motivate students from the outside with rewards and punishments. The results speak for themselves. Some students do well. Some do horribly. Most comply, but seldom do they do their best work. To bolster motivation and achievement, we have seen the proliferation of high-stakes tests, the ultimate weapon in the reward/punishment arsenal. High-stakes testing is the standard-bearer of an external control orientation, predicated on the assumption that raising standards and threatening students that they will not graduate will improve learning. While the intent is positive (improving academic achievement), the results of high-stakes testing need to be examined.

What does the research tell us about efforts to improve education based on external motivation? In "The Effects of High-Stakes Testing on Student Motivation and Learning," Amrein and Berliner (2003) come to the following conclusion:

> The evidence shows that such tests actually decrease student motivation and increase the proportion of students who leave school early. Further, student achievement in the 18 high-stakes testing states has not improved on a range of measures. . . . Researchers have found that when rewards and sanctions are attached to performance on tests, students become *less* intrinsically motivated to learn and less likely to engage in critical thinking. (p. 32)

Even though students are doing better on the high-stakes tests (a function of teachers "teaching to the test"), they have failed to improve with regard to other measures, such as the National Assessment of Educational Progress. The dropout rate is increasing, especially in states where the stakes are the highest. As Amrein and Berliner (2003) noted,

> We calculated that 88 percent of the states with high school graduation tests have higher dropout rates than do states without graduation tests. In 62 percent of these states, dropout rates increased in comparison with the rest of the nation after the state implemented high-stakes graduation exams. In addition, the top 10 states with the weakest graduation ratios all administered high-stakes tests over the years for which data were available. (p. 33)

With high-stakes testing here to stay for the foreseeable future, it is imperative to help students see the relevance of what they are asked to learn and to create a shared picture of success. A continued reliance on the reward/punishment model will lead to even more students dropping out and increased cynicism among those who stay and "succeed." In the face of the threats implicit in high-stakes testing, it is more important than ever to create classrooms and schools that are need-satisfying, are collaborative, are engaging, and foster internal motivation.

We have been unsuccessful in our attempt to motivate more students to achieve academically and behave responsibly because we have based our efforts on the mistaken belief that people can be externally motivated to do their best work. In truth, we are motivated from within.

The good news is that we can create learning environments that foster the motivation that makes education a joyful enterprise. Internal control psychology teaches us that we are driven to connect, to be competent, to make choices, to have fun, and to be safe. Structure a classroom and school where those five needs are regularly met, and you will inspire motivation that fuels academic excellence and exemplary behavior.

Teachers around the country are discovering the effectiveness of internal control and motivation. We work hard to attain what we value. We create internal pictures of what we want and do everything we can to achieve self-selected goals. When others attempt to externally control us, we are motivated to free ourselves from their controlling efforts. Conversely, when students and teachers create a shared vision of what is to be learned, students are internally motivated to engage in high-quality academic work. In such an environment, achievement increases and behavioral problems decrease. When educators apply internal control psychology, they love their jobs and their students thrive.

In *Activating the Desire to Learn*, you have been given a comprehensive overview of internal control psychology. You have seen that this new model of human behavior and motivation is repeatedly validated by research. When internal control psychology is consistently applied, students flourish academically and their behavior improves. You have heard from teachers, counselors, administrators, and students. I encourage you to join me and others committed to transforming our schools. Let's give our children an education that is engaging, collaborative, and inspiring—one that gives students the motivation to demonstrate high-quality academic work. Let's create classrooms and schools that reflect a fundamental truth: We are motivated from the inside out.

Bibliography

Amrein, A., & Berliner, D. (2003). The effects of high-stakes testing on student motivation and learning. *Educational Leadership, 60*(5), 32–37.

Bryk, A., & Schneider, B. (2003). Trust in schools: A core resource for school reform. *Educational Leadership, 60*(6), 40–44.

Buck, N. (2000). *Peaceful parenting.* San Diego, CA: Black Forest Press.

Crawford, D., Bodine, R., & Hoglund, R. (1993). *The school for quality learning: Managing the school and classroom the Deming way.* Champaign, IL: Research Press.

Dyer, W. (1998). *Wisdom of the ages: A modern master brings eternal truth into everyday life.* New York: Harper-Collins.

Elkind, D. (1981). *The hurried child: Growing up too fast, too soon.* Reading, MA: Addison-Wesley.

Elkind, D. (1984). *All grown up and no place to go: Teenagers in crisis.* Reading, MA: Addison-Wesley.

Elkind, D. (1987). *Miseducation: Preschoolers at risk.* New York: Knopf.

Erwin, J. (2004). *The classroom of choice: Giving students what they need and getting what you want.* Alexandria, VA: Association for Supervision and Curriculum Development.

Frankl, V. (1959). *Man's search for meaning.* Boston: Beacon Press.

Gardner, H. (1993). *Frames of mind: The theory of multiple intelligences.* New York: BasicBooks.

Glasser, W. (1990). *The quality school: Managing students without coercion.* New York: Perennial Library.

Glasser, W. (1992). *The quality school teacher.* Canoga Park, CA: The William Glasser Institute.

Glasser, W. (1998). *Choice theory: A new psychology of personal freedom.* New York: HarperCollins Publishers.

Glasser, W. (2000). *Every student can succeed.* Chula Vista, CA: Black Forest Press.

Good, E. P., Grumley, J., & Roy, S. (2003). *A connected school.* Chapel Hill, NC: New View Publications.

Gossen, D., & Anderson, J. (1995). *Creating the conditions: Leadership for quality schools.* Chapel Hill, NC: New View Publications.

Greene, B. (1994). *New paradigms for creating quality schools.* Chapel Hill, NC: New View Publications.

Jensen, E. (1995). *Brain-based learning and teaching.* Del Mar, CA: Turning Point Publishing.

Jensen, E. (1996). *Completing the puzzle: The brain-compatible approach to learning.* Del Mar, CA: Turning Point Publishing.

Jensen, E. (1998). *Teaching with the brain in mind.* Alexandria, VA: Association for Supervision and Curriculum Development.

Johnson, D., Johnson, R., & Holubec, E. (1993). *Circles of learning: Cooperation in the classroom* (4th ed.). Edina, MN: Interaction Book Co.

Kim, K. (2002). The effect of a reality therapy program on the responsibility for elementary school children in Korea. *International Journal of Reality Therapy, 22*(2), 30–33.

Kim, R., & Hwang, M. (2001). The effect of internal control and achievement motivation in group counseling based on reality therapy. *International Journal of Reality Therapy, 20*(2), 12–25.

Kohn, A. (1993). *Punished by rewards: The trouble with gold stars, incentive plans, A's, praise, and other bribes.* Boston: Houghton Mifflin.

Kohn, A. (1999). *The schools our children deserve: Moving beyond traditional classrooms and "tougher standards."* Boston: Houghton Mifflin.

Leachman, G., & Victor, D. (2003). Student-led class meetings. *Educational Leadership, 60*(6), 64–68.

Lickona, T. (1983). *Raising good children: Helping your child through the stages of moral development.* New York: Bantam Books.

Ludwig, S., & Mentley, K. (1997). *Quality is the key: Stories from Huntington Woods School.* Wyoming, MI: KWM Educational Services.

Marzano, R., & Marzano, J. (2003). The key to classroom management. *Educational Leadership, 61*(1), 6–13.

Pease, A., & Law, J. (2000). CT/RT/LM and student conduct. *International Journal of Reality Therapy, 19*(2), 4–9.

Powers, W. (1998). *Making sense of behavior: The meaning of control.* New Canaan, CT: Benchmark Publications.

Rogers, S., Ludington, J., & Graham, S. (1997). *Motivation and learning: A teacher's guide to building excitement for learning and igniting the drive for quality.* Evergreen, CO: Peak Learning Systems.

Schaps, E. (2003). Creating a school community. *Educational Leadership, 60*(6), 31–33.

Schmoker, M. (2003). First things first: Demystifying data analysis. *Educational Leadership, 60*(5), 22–24.

Skinner, B. F. (1948). *Walden two.* New York: MacMillan.

Strong, R., Silver, H., Perini, M., & Tuculescu, G. (2003). Boredom and its opposite. *Educational Leadership, 61*(1), 24–29.

Sullo, R. (1989). *Teach them to be happy.* Chapel Hill, NC: New View Publications.

Sullo, R. (1997). *Inspiring quality in your school: From theory to practice.* West Haven, CT: NEA Professional Library.

Sullo, R. (1999). *The inspiring teacher: New beginnings for the 21st century.* Annapolis, MD: NEA Professional Library.

Wigle, S., & Sandoval, P. (2000). Change and challenges in a school of education: Choice theory as an effective leadership paradigm. *International Journal of Reality Therapy, 20*(1), 4–9.

Index

About the Author

 An educator for over 30 years, Bob Sullo has been an English teacher, adjustment counselor, school psychologist, and administrator. Over the course of his career, Bob has worked with both regular education and special education students from preK through graduation in elementary, middle, and high school. He is currently a housemaster at Plymouth South Middle School in Plymouth, Massachusetts.

Bob has worked with thousands of educators and parents, conducting staff development workshops and parent workshops in more than two dozen states. His presentations focus on the importance of internal motivation and how to inspire students to do high-quality work in a joyful environment. Bob's previous books include *Teach Them to Be Happy* (New View Publications, 1989), *Inspiring Quality in Your School: From Theory to Practice* (NEA Professional Library, 1997), and *The Inspiring Teacher: New Beginnings for the 21st Century* (NEA Professional Library, 1999).

Bob and his wife, Laurie, live in Sandwich, Massachusetts. He can be reached at P.O. Box 1336, Sandwich, MA 02563. Phone: 774-283-1186. For training or consulting, visit Bob's Web site at http://www.internalmotivation.net or e-mail him at bob@internalmotivation.net.

Related ASCD Resources: Motivating Students

At the time of publication, the following ASCD resources were available; for the most up-to-date information about ASCD resources, go to www.ascd.org. ASCD stock numbers are noted in parentheses.

Books

Accountability for Learning: How Teachers and School Leaders Can Take Charge, by Douglas B. Reeves (#104004)

Activating and Engaging Habits of Mind, by Arthur L. Costa and Bena Kallick (#100033)

The Big Picture: Education Is Everyone's Business, by Dennis Littky and Samantha Grabelle (#104438)

Multimedia

Emotional Intelligence Professional Inquiry Kit, by Pam Robbins and Jane Scott (#997146)

Project-Based Learning with Multimedia (CD-ROM), by the San Mateo County Office of Education (#502117)

Video

High Schools at Work: Creating Student-Centered Learning Three Tape Series with Facilitator's Guide (#406117)

Educating Everybody's Children, Tape 4: Increasing Interest, Motivation, and Engagement (#400225)

For more information, visit us on the World Wide Web (http://www.ascd.org), send an e-mail message to member@ascd.org, call the ASCD Service Center (1-800-933-ASCD or 703-578-9600, then press 2), send a fax to 703-575-5400, or write to Information Services, ASCD, 1703 N. Beauregard St., Alexandria, VA 22311-1714 USA.